D1153151

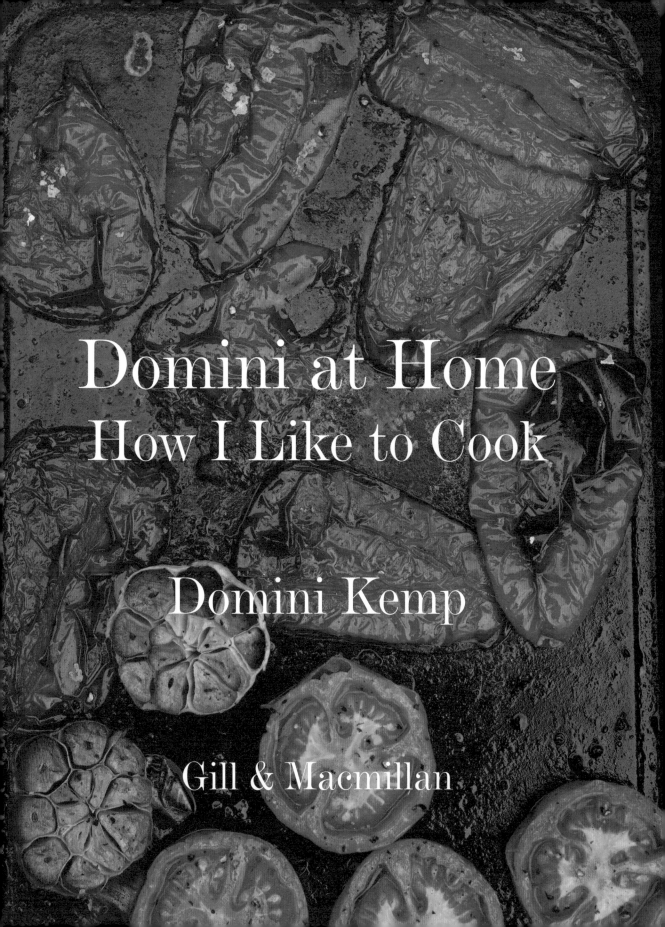

Domini at Home
How I Like to Cook

Domini Kemp

Gill & Macmillan

Gill & Macmillan
Hume Avenue, Park West, Dublin 12
with associated companies throughout the world
www.gillmacmillan.ie

© Domini Kemp 2012

978 07171 5443 2

Photography: Joanne Murphy
Styling by: Orla Nelligan, Carly Horan
Food styling: Domini Kemp, Paul Kavanagh
Editing: Gillian Fallon
Print origination in Ireland by Slick Fish Design
Indexed by Helen Litton
Printed by Printer Trento Srl, Italy

Props: Avoca; Eden Home & Garden; Meadows & Byrne; Article; Marks & Spencer; Cath Kidston;
House of Fraser; The Blue Door; Historic Interiors

The paper used in this book is made from the wood pulp of managed forests. For every tree felled,
at least one tree is planted, thereby renewing natural resources.

A CIP catalogue record for this book is available from the British Library.

introduction

Do we really need another cookbook? Yes. And not just because I've written one.

I believe that anything that helps us to cook at home regularly and to avoid relying on ready meals or takeaways – and that gets us interested in cooking – is worth doing. And by interested in cooking, I do mean cooking, cooking. Not just ogling at books, but actually getting out your knife and chopping board, turning on the oven and making some dinner.

It's what we should be looking for from a cookbook nowadays, because certainly our requirements are somewhat simpler. How to do more with less seems to be how we're all living each day. But less in terms of cost should not imply 'mean', especially in terms of flavour and satisfaction. Less really can be more if it means practical, flexible recipes that will draw people to sit around the table, eat good food and talk.

I am dogged in my pursuit of how to get the best flavour out of food, whether it is a simple sandwich and bowl of soup or a five-course fine-dining banquet for a grand occasion. Flavours, science and technique are things that most people associate with professionals, and think have little bearing on how they do things at home. But taking the basics and introducing them into your everyday routine is something I'm keen to impart, especially when it's pretty straightforward.

Take the everyday task of making toast, for instance. When you pile it all up on a plate, it goes soggy. Toast racks help prevent this. Although not all of us may be posh enough to have a toast rack, just think about this when you're roasting some butternut squash in the oven or sautéing some mushrooms. If you overload things – whether in a roasting tin or a frying pan – you create steam, so ingredients take ages to generate enough heat to crisp up around the edges. They remain soggy and we can't get that extra bit of caramelisation and oomph into our dish. Thinking about these things – even just a tiny bit – will help you to get better results.

As well as coming up with my own ideas, my aim is to find recipes that sound great, then to pare them back and strip them down, eliminating unnecessary steps and simplifying what can initially seem daunting. I hope this is never disrespectful to the inventor of the original recipe, although the idea of any recipe being truly original is usually limited to only a handful of mega-chefs. Even a picture of a dish will trip some culinary switch in my head. After that, I pursue the shortest, tastiest and most efficient route possible to re-create the dish in a way that makes sense to me. Call it plagiarism, call it lazy, call it practical. I'm sure it's a little of all the above. But more than anything, it's how I like to cook.

contents

fancy casual

I'm a devil for inviting people over for dinner and leaving everything
– including cooking, shopping and the inviting part – until the very
last minute.

Because of this relaxed (read slap-dash) approach to casual suppers,
I'm also quite happy to get some bread, a few types of cheese (like
Corleggy or Knockdrinna or Glebe Brethan) and make a big green
salad. It's the type of meal I'd happily eat every day and is the ultimate
in 'good' fast food. It's the perfect type of supper for sharing and ideal
for lots of nattering and a glass or two of wine. Isn't that what supper
with friends is all about?

But sometimes you want to make a bit of effort, and that's what this
chapter is for. It's about having a few dishes up your sleeve that will
ensure your reputation as host isn't in tatters (which mine occasionally
is). One or two show-stoppers will keep the naysayers at bay and the
smart guests asking for second helpings, and therefore another invite.

Gourmet fancy pants burgers, ultimate oven fries, spicy tomato and horseradish ketchup

Fancy pants burgers

Serves 4

650 g sirloin steak, minced

150 g pork belly, minced

Good few splashes Worcestershire sauce

2 tbsp fresh thyme leaves

2 tsp wholegrain mustard

1 tbsp tomato ketchup

Salt and pepper

This is my favourite recipe for burgers, but these babies should be served only to your very best friends as they're made with minced-up sirloin steak (which is why you need to be choosy about your guests) and a bit of pork belly. You get fantastic flavour plus some extra fat: two important elements in creating a great burger.

Mix the meats with the rest of the ingredients in a bowl using a fork or even your hands, which you'll need to wash well, both before and after. Shape into four or five burgers (you could probably make a sixth if you had to be stingy) and chill for an hour. Cook on a barbecue or chargrill. Do cook them through fully, as they contain raw pork – so no medium rare, I'm sorry to say. And 2 tablespoons of thyme leaves seems like a lot, but trust me, they taste great.

Top with your favourite buns, pickles, red onion, lettuce, tomato – the works. Whatever you fancy.

Ultimate oven fries

3 big rooster potatoes

100 ml olive oil

Salt and freshly ground black pepper

The fries are the ultimate companions. The recipe comes from a wonderfully 'nerdy' US food magazine called Cook's Illustrated. Actually it's pretty fantastic, but it's text-heavy and picture-light, full of long diatribes about testing the world's favourite recipes. It's aimed at all cooks from the mildly curious to the very annoying (like me) who want to know, as they say in their intro, why 'bad things happen to good recipes'. It almost sounds like some sort of CSI culinary whodunit, full of interesting facts and observations. Their 1,400-word methodology for oven chips has been whittled down here to a few lines. These are a joy to eat but, for once, I urge you to follow the recipe to the letter! The devil really is in the detail.

Preheat the oven to 220°C and put the shelf as low as you can, without resting it on the oven floor.

Don't bother peeling the spuds; just cut them into thin finger-width sticks. Soak them in a bowl of hot tap water for 10 minutes, then drain and pat dry on kitchen paper until very dry. In a bowl, toss them with the oil and lots of salt and pepper. Lay them out on a heavy baking sheet in one single layer. Cover with tinfoil and bake for 15 to 20 minutes. Then remove the tinfoil and carefully turn the fries over. They should be starting to go a lovely golden brown on the bottom. Bake them for a further 7 to 10 minutes until crisp, golden brown and soft and delicious inside. Season well and serve with the ketchup.

2 kg slightly over-ripe tomatoes

2 small white onions

1 large cooking apple

Big piece fresh horseradish, peeled

Big piece ginger, peeled

Few cloves garlic, peeled

1 tbsp tomato purée

6 cloves

1 tsp mustard seeds

1 cinnamon stick

1 tsp celery seeds

1 tbsp flaky sea salt OR small tsp fine sea salt

Few splashes Tabasco sauce

250 ml white wine vinegar

250 g light brown sugar

Spicy tomato and horseradish ketchup

The accompanying home-made horseradish ketchup oozes flavour. And while I'm sure it would be much nicer made with super red, ripe and juicy tomatoes in the height of summer, I'm happy to stick it in here because I used fairly grim tomatoes and they worked out really well, regardless.

Roughly chop the tomatoes and chuck into a large heavy-based saucepan. Peel the onions and apples, finely dice and add to the tomatoes. Finely chop the horseradish and ginger, and add to the tomatoes along with the garlic and all the other ingredients, except for half the vinegar and all the sugar. Simmer slowly for an hour. Stir occasionally and mush up. Pass through a sieve into a clean saucepan, discard the debris and add the rest of the vinegar and the sugar. Cook gently for another 30 to 40 minutes until the ketchup is thick. Season and allow to cool. Refrigerate and keep for up to a month in a jar in the fridge.

Posh chicken Kiev

Serves 2

100 g butter, softened
Handful basil leaves
Handful flat leaf parsley
1 tbsp toasted pine nuts
1 tbsp Parmesan cheese, grated
4 cloves garlic, peeled and crushed
Salt and pepper
2 large chicken breasts, skinless
Big knob butter
2 tbsp sunflower oil

Crumb coating:
100 g breadcrumbs
30 g Parmesan cheese, grated
1 egg, beaten
2 tbsp flour

One of my favourite food writers is a gentlewoman called Ruth Watson, who also does a decent sideline as a TV presenter. Her writing is as appealing as her TV persona: no nonsense and, at times, very amusing. As Watson puts it so perfectly: when entertaining, deep-fat frying anything means that you always emerge from the kitchen 'shiny and faintly hysterical', so finishing this dish in the oven means you can instead emerge victorious and matt. The cos salad with mustard dressing (see page 90) is a perfect accompaniment.

In a food processor, whizz the butter, herbs, pine nuts, Parmesan cheese and garlic with plenty of salt and pepper until smooth. Wrap the butter mixture in clingfilm, roll out into a sausage shape and freeze. This amount makes lots of butter – more than you need here – but it's awkward to whizz less butter.

When the butter is good and cold, make a horizontal slit in each chicken breast and stuff with a good amount of butter. Close it up as well as you can, wash your hands really well and then chill the breasts down until you are ready to finish cooking.

Preheat the oven to 170°C.

Prepare the coating: mix the breadcrumbs and Parmesan cheese together and season well and spread out on a plate. Have the egg beaten and ready in a bowl. On a second plate, spread out the flour and, again, season very well.

Dunk the chicken as follows: flour, egg, flour, egg, breadcrumb. Chill again for 30 minutes and then shallow fry in a large non-stick saucepan in the knob of butter and the sunflower oil. When the chicken is golden brown on both sides, transfer to the oven and bake for 7 to 10 minutes.

Serve with an extra knob of the garlic and herb butter.

Tomato jelly with basil goat's cheese

Serves 4

200 ml water

2 genuinely heaped tsp agar flakes

500 g very ripe tomatoes

1 good tsp flaky sea salt

1 good tsp caster sugar

Pinch chilli flakes

125 g soft goat's cheese

1 tbsp crème fraîche OR cream

1 garlic clove, peeled and crushed

Few basil leaves, finely sliced

Salt and pepper

British chef Simon Hopkinson's cooking is very butch and very protein-driven, but one of his recent books, *The Vegetarian Option*, offers exactly what it says on the cover. The recipe below is based on his version and, like most of his recipes, it doesn't disappoint.

With a real feel of summer, this tomato jelly is incredibly easy to make and would be a really good dinner-party dish. Agar melts at around 80°C and sets at around 35°C, which means that when you're cooling the jelly over ice, it doesn't take too long before you notice it becoming a bit viscous in texture. This is the point at which you pour it into your glasses or ramekins, as once it sets, you don't really want to decant and ruin the pristine look of it all.

Put the water in a small stainless-steel saucepan. Sprinkle the agar flakes on top (as if feeding goldfish) and don't stir. Make sure you use flakes instead of powder. Bring gently to a simmer. At this stage, you can gently swirl around the water so that all the flakes fully sink. Simmer for a few minutes, very gently, while you roughly chop the tomatoes, which you should add in, along with the salt, sugar and chilli flakes. At this stage you can stir and mix well, bringing it up to a bit of a boil again and mushing the tomatoes up. Then strain the tomato juice into a clean bowl and discard the pulp. Allow it to start cooling, while you get the goat's cheese mixture sorted, and prepare an ice bath – just a bowl or roasting tin with some ice cubes and water – which your bowl of tomato juice can sit on to cool down.

Mix the goat's cheese, crème fraîche/cream, garlic and basil with a spatula and season really well. Then divide it between four glasses or ramekins. When you're ready to go, start chilling the tomato over the ice bath, mixing with a wooden spoon. After a few minutes, you may notice that it's become slightly viscous. Taste it and make sure you're happy with the seasoning. When it's getting close to tepid, pour the tomato sauce on top of the goat's cheese. Then chill down and serve later. They'll only take an hour or so to set.

Serve with plenty of hot buttered toast and green leaves.

Venison stew

Serves 6

2 tbsp olive oil

2 onions, peeled and finely chopped

1 kg venison, diced

Few sprigs thyme

Salt and pepper

300 g mushrooms, chopped

½ bottle red wine

500 ml vegetable stock OR water

4 cloves garlic, peeled and sliced

50 g dried cranberries

200 g Jerusalem artichokes, peeled and cut in half

This is a really good-for-you, meaty stew. I use haunch of venison for this, but really anything will do. It is nutritionally sound because, like most red meat, venison is a source of protein, zinc, iron and selenium. The good news is that it's also lower in fat and calories than beef; in fact, venison has about one-third of the fat. Yes, there is half a bottle of vino in there, but this recipe makes enough to feed six, and after cooking the stew for a few hours, there will be no alcohol left in the pot – just good flavours.

In a large saucepan, heat the olive oil and sweat the onions over a high heat until they just start to colour. Keeping the heat up high, add the venison and let it brown. After 5 minutes, add the thyme and season. Chuck in the mushrooms and try to get some colour on them. Then add the wine, stock/water, garlic and cranberries. Bring up to a simmer, cover with a lid and cook for 30 minutes. Add the artichokes, cover again, but only partially, and stew for at least another hour.

Taste, season and, once the venison is tender, cool slightly and serve with brown rice if you're good or buttery mash if you're bad.

Smoked eel and bacon salad

Serves 4 (starter)

1 head frisée lettuce

Squeeze lemon juice

Olive oil

200 g smoked eel fillets, thinly sliced

8 thin rashers, grilled until crisp

Bunch chives, finely chopped

Butter dressing:

1 shallot, peeled and chopped

2 tbsp white wine vinegar

2 tbsp white wine

2 tbsp water

125 g unsalted butter, cut into cubes

To enjoy the delicacy of smoked eel, I highly recommend buying a pack of smoked eel fillets from Ummera Smokehouse (based in Cork). This is definitely a better option than fishing for them out in the Sargasso Sea (where it's thought they are born) – Lord knows what might happen to you out there in the Bermuda Triangle! You can make this delicious salad, adapted from a Rowley Leigh recipe, using the Ummera smoked bacon as well. If you don't fancy the eel, use smoked salmon instead.

First, make the dressing: heat up everything except the butter in a small saucepan and reduce until you have one tablespoon of liquid left. Over a low heat, whisk in the butter very gradually. Add a few splashes of water, every now and then, if it looks like it might split. Season and set aside.

Toss the frisée with a little olive oil and lemon juice. Arrange on a big platter with slices of the eel and broken-up pieces of the rashers. Spoon over the dressing and sprinkle with chives.

Lime, chilli and ginger prawns

Serves 6–10 (canapés)

20 tiger prawns, cooked and peeled

2 cloves garlic, peeled and crushed

Big piece ginger, peeled and grated

1 tbsp sweet chilli sauce

3 tbsp soy sauce

1 tbsp honey

1 tbsp sunflower oil

Juice of 4 limes

When it comes to entertaining for large numbers, especially at short notice (like at Christmas), it's good to have a few things up your sleeve – and in your freezer. Frozen tiger prawns should be part of everyone's freezer arsenal. Raw ones are great but sometimes they need to be de-veined, which is a bit of a chore when you're stuck for time. They do well if marinated and then grilled, as in this recipe, and will quickly disappear when hungry guests appear. All you need is some napkins for sticky fingers.

Marinate the prawns in all the other ingredients for about 30 minutes and then grill on a baking tray on a high heat until sizzling hot and sticky. Cook for a bit longer if they are raw, but they won't take long, either way. Decant onto a large serving platter and serve whilst hot.

If you find that you've lots of juice from the limes, then you can always strain the prawns after marinating them and reduce down the marinade by half in a frying pan by boiling rapidly. This makes a 'stickier' glaze for the prawns and works quite well. Then you simply pour this back over the prawns before grilling to ensure they go sticky and caramelised as opposed to stewing under the grill.

Roast pork with prune, pine nut and spinach stuffing

Serves 4–6

1 pork fillet

1 onion, peeled and diced

2 tbsp olive oil

4 smoked streaky bacon rashers, diced

2 cloves garlic, peeled and crushed

150 g baby spinach

130 g stoned and chopped prunes

2 tbsp pine nuts, toasted

Salt and pepper

4–6 slices Parma ham

8–10 shallots, peeled

Big knob butter

1 tbsp redcurrant jelly

It can be easy to over-cater on big occasions or family gatherings, so if your aim is to have just one meat dish and as little left over as possible, this very tasty roast pork recipe may just do the trick.

Preheat the oven to 180°C.

Slice the pork fillet in half (lengthways), but not all the way through. Put it between two sheets of clingfilm and bash with a rolling pin to turn it into one large rectangle of flattened fillet.

To make the stuffing: sweat the onions in the olive oil until soft. Turn up the heat, add the rashers and fry until brown and crisp. Add the garlic, spinach, prunes and pine nuts and sauté until the spinach wilts. Keep the heat turned up so that any water from the spinach evaporates. Season and set aside to cool.

Once the stuffing is completely cold, you can stuff the pork and leave overnight, ready to cook. If you're cooking it straightaway then it's okay to stuff the pork while the stuffing is still warm. Spoon the stuffing in a straight line right down the middle of the pork, then roll the pork up and wrap it with the Parma ham. Tie at intervals with string. Roast in a roasting tray for about 20 minutes.

Meanwhile, heat up the butter and sweat the shallots in a saucepan until golden brown. Take the pork out of the oven, add the buttery shallots to the roasting tray and smear the pork with the redcurrant jelly. Baste with the juices, season with black pepper and roast for about another 20 minutes. So, cook the pork for 40 minutes in total.

Leave to rest for 10 minutes before carving. Serve with the shallots and pan juices.

Smoked salmon pâté and cucumber salad

Another part of my arsenal of recipes under the umbrella of 'emergency catering', this salmon pâté is lovely with cucumber salad on top and is perfect spooned onto some toast or brown bread.

Use trimmings, good stuff or any combination of smoked fish. Don't get hung up on exact quantities for the cream cheese or salmon. It's a rough recipe and 50 grams here or there won't make too much difference. Very handy when you're under pressure to produce something tasty, and fast. Extra lemon juice and some chopped chives are good accessories if you don't have time to make the cucumber salad.

Smoked salmon pâté

Serves 8 (starter) to 15 (canapés)

500 g smoked salmon

400 g cream cheese

100 ml crème fraîche

Zest and juice of 2 lemons

Good pinch cayenne pepper

Big bunch dill, finely chopped

Lots of black pepper and a pinch of salt

In a food processor, whizz the salmon on pulse with the cream cheese and crème fraîche. Stir in the remaining ingredients and season to taste. Chill until ready to serve on hot toast or brown bread with the cucumber salad. Keeps pretty well if covered in the fridge for a few days.

Cucumber salad

2 cucumbers

1 red onion

Bunch flat leaf parsley

Dressing:
Salt

2 tbsp rice wine vinegar OR cider vinegar

2 tsp caster sugar

2 tbsp olive oil

Big piece ginger, peeled and very finely chopped

1 clove garlic, peeled and crushed

Mix the ingredients for the dressing together by shaking them in a jar. Peel and finely slice the cucumbers and red onion, and chop the parsley. Mix the salad items together, add the dressing, mix and leave to sit for an hour. Season well and serve. Pickled cucumber can be a bit too strong for some people's liking, but this one hits the spot nicely.

Lamb stew with prunes, maple and chilli, and sweet potato purée

Serves 6

2 tbsp olive oil

1 boned leg of lamb, diced into bite-sized chunks

Salt and pepper

3 large onions, peeled and sliced

Big piece ginger, peeled and diced

6 cloves garlic, peeled and chopped

2 chillies, finely chopped

Big bunch coriander

1.5 litres water

2 x 400 g tins chopped tomatoes

Few bay leaves

100 ml soy sauce

3 tbsp maple syrup

200 g prunes, roughly chopped

Zest and juice of 2 limes

Spice mix:
2 cinnamon sticks, broken up

1 tsp coriander seeds

1 tsp cumin seeds

1 tsp fennel seeds

1 tsp fenugreek

5 whole cardamoms

2 star anise

2 cloves

6 big sweet potatoes

2 chillies, roughly chopped

Salt and pepper

75 g butter

Good glug olive oil

Good few splashes soy sauce

Good squeeze maple syrup

When, two years ago, some very unsubtle hinting on my part resulted in one superstar friend (thanks, Livia!) gifting me with a longed-for pestle and mortar, I trawled my cache of cookbooks for dishes that would allow me to try out my new gizmo. One of the best is this lamb dish, simplified from a Skye Gyngell recipe. I love a blend of spicy, salty and sweet – unless you're just going for a very butch, meaty and alcohol-based kick from a classic, such as beef bourguignon or a beef and Guinness stew. The soft sweet potato purée is perfect with it.

Lamb stew with prunes, maple and chilli

In a heavy-based saucepan, heat the olive oil, brown the lamb well and season with plenty of salt and pepper. This should take a good 10 minutes. At this stage, you can drain some of the fat off if too much has been rendered from the lamb. Add the onions, ginger, garlic and chillies and sweat for another 10 minutes so that they start to caramelise a little.

Meanwhile, prepare your spice mix. Heat all the spices in a non-stick frying pan until just starting to smoke. Remove from the heat and grind up in a grinder or with a pestle and mortar or in my old ignorant way – with a rolling pin and a cup. When it's ready and ground down, add to the lamb. Mix well so all the meat is well coated.

Chop the stems off the coriander and add the stems to the lamb along with the water, tomatoes and bay leaves. Mix well and simmer with a lid half on, for about an hour. Check it every now and then – if too much liquid is evaporating, then add some more water or cover fully with the lid. After about an hour, add the rest of the ingredients and cook for another 30 minutes or so. Taste again and adjust the seasoning if necessary. Let it sit for a while before dishing out. Needless to say, it tastes even better the next day. Serve with the sweet potato purée and coriander leaves on top.

Sweet potato purée

Peel the spuds, cut them into chunks and place them in a large saucepan of cold water. Bring up to the boil and simmer until tender. Drain and then blend in a food processor or just mash with the rest of the ingredients. Regular spuds go too starchy if you put them in a food processor, but sweet potatoes are a little less precious.

Seared scallops and crème fraîche with sweet chilli sauce

I am very partial to scallops generally, but if I'm being honest, the whole raison d'être of this dish is the delicious sweet chilli sauce from Kiwi mega-chef Peter Gordon, which would happily glide over grilled chicken or other fish such as monkfish or salmon. I could also see it as a perfect dunking sauce for chargrilled prawns. So many commercial brands of sweet chilli sauce are sickly sweet, bright red syrups with chopped up bits of chilli blobbing around. This sauce, on the other hand, is fragrant, floral and much less one-dimensional in flavour. It makes enough to fill a large jam jar and will keep in the fridge for about two weeks. If seasonality is important to you, remember that in Ireland scallops are fished around the coast in winter and spring.

Seared scallops and crème fraîche

Serves 3–5

15 scallops

Bunch rocket

200 ml crème fraîche

Salt and pepper

Squeeze lime juice

1 tbsp sunflower oil

Heat the oil and sear the scallops for a minute or two on each side. Season lightly and then place on top of some rocket. Season the crème fraîche with the lime juice, salt and pepper, then drizzle on top of the scallops. Add a few blobs of the sweet chilli sauce.

Sweet chilli sauce

250 g caster sugar

10 cloves garlic, peeled

4 red chillies

½ whole piece of ginger, peeled and roughly chopped

8 lime leaves

3 lemon grass stems, roughly chopped

Big bunch coriander

100 ml cider vinegar

3 tbsp fish sauce

3 tbsp soy sauce

Put 200 ml water in a heavy-based saucepan and add the sugar. Don't stir; just heat it up until the sugar dissolves and then turn up the heat and gently simmer until the sugar turns a nice caramel colour. Meanwhile, whizz all the other ingredients together to form a slightly chunky paste. You don't want it as smooth as soup, but you do need to make light work of the hunks of ginger, garlic and lemongrass. Take the caramel off the heat and add the paste carefully (getting splattered with hot caramel is not nice). Whisk gently, then put back on the heat for a few minutes to help all those flavours to open up. Allow to cool, and drizzle over the scallops or whatever you like.

Lime and mint chicken parcels

Serves 4

4–6 chicken breasts, skin removed, roughly chopped

1 litre water

2 tbsp fish sauce

2 tsp granulated sugar

Big piece ginger, peeled and thinly chopped

1 chilli, deseeded and finely sliced

2 cloves garlic, peeled and finely sliced

Bunch mint leaves

Bunch basil leaves

Bunch coriander

1 cucumber, deseeded and finely sliced

Juice of 4 limes

Splash soy sauce

Splash sweet chilli sauce

1 small red onion, peeled and thinly sliced

Bunch spring onions, finely chopped

Splash of sunflower oil

Salt and pepper

2 baby gem lettuces

2 tbsp pistachios, lightly toasted

These gorgeous little parcels of spiced minced chicken are fragrant, fresh and delicious. Perfect as a starter for a big group.

In a food processor, pulse the chicken so that the meat becomes finely minced. If you don't have a food processor, then chop finely. In a large saucepan, heat the water along with the fish sauce, sugar, ginger, chilli and garlic. When it comes to the boil, add the chicken. Bring back to the boil and then reduce the heat to a simmer. Break up the chicken from forming clumps with a wooden spoon. Cook for a few minutes and then turn the heat off and allow the chicken to cook gently in the residual heat for another 10 minutes with the lid on. Mix well and check to see the meat is thoroughly cooked. Allow to cool. Strain and keep the cooking liquid for cooking rice or noodles.

Meanwhile, chop the herbs and mix with the cucumber, lime juice, soy sauce, sweet chilli sauce, red onion, spring onions, sunflower oil and some black pepper. Check the seasoning.

When the chicken has cooled down, spoon some of the chicken mix into each baby gem leaf, top with the herb and cucumber sauce and serve with a sprinkle of chopped pistachios on top.

Niçoise salad with salsa verde and sundried tomato tapenade

Anyone who's been to the south of France will be all too familiar with the plethora of Niçoise salads on offer in every café and bistro. In warm weather, it's one of my favourite salads to make, and although it seems that a traditional or authentic Niçoise is not supposed to have any cooked vegetables in it (so, no potatoes or green beans then) I love that there are about five million 'authentic' versions. Nowadays it's up for grabs what you put in it. The version here is pretty hearty and takes a 'more the merrier' approach.

For the dressing, I opted for a really good salsa verde and a divine sundried tomato tapenade drummed up by my sister Peaches. To serve, either lay the salad out almost like a giant crudités platter or chuck everything into a bowl and toss with the salsa verde and another lick of olive oil. It makes a great supper. Feel free to amend the ingredients as necessary. This is an ad hoc salad, and would also be delicious with smoked trout.

Niçoise salad

Serves 4 (main course) to 8 (side dish)

1 red onion

2 tbsp red wine vinegar

500 g baby new potatoes

180 g green beans

4 tomatoes

Few drizzles olive oil

Few splashes balsamic vinegar

Few pinches sugar

Salt and pepper

4 eggs

1 fennel

2 heads chicory

250 g cherry tomatoes

250 g olives, stoned

1 radicchio OR baby gem lettuce

2 x 250 g tins tuna

Preheat the oven to 200°C.

Slice the red onion very thinly and leave to marinate in the red wine vinegar while you prepare the new potatoes. Boil the potatoes until tender, drain and set aside to cool. Then slice in half and keep at room temperature. Slice the 4 tomatoes in half, put in a roasting tin and drizzle with a bit of olive oil and balsamic vinegar. Season with salt, pepper and sugar. Roast for about 15 to 30 minutes until they've started to shrivel up and caramelise, then set aside to cool. Blanch the green beans in boiling water for one minute, drain and rinse until cold.

Cook the eggs (straight from the fridge) in cold water, which you slowly bring up to the boil and then simmer for about 3 minutes for soft-boiled eggs. If the eggs are at room temperature, you can probably do it for 2 minutes. But I appreciate that many people like their eggs cooked differently, so decide how long you want to cook them for and then drain and rinse under a cold tap. Crack the shells, peel and set the eggs aside.

Slice the fennel, lettuce, chicory and cherry tomatoes. Roughly chop the olives. Pour the marinated onions onto the potatoes and mix. Season them well. Drain the tuna and arrange on a platter. Serve with the sundried tomato tapenade and salsa verde, or else mix and toss all the ingredients together, using a little extra olive oil if necessary.

Salsa verde

Large handful flat leaf parsley

Smaller handful mint leaves

4 tsp capers

Lots of black pepper

2 good tsp Dijon mustard

Good pinch sugar

5 tbsp olive oil

Salt

Blitz all the ingredients in a food processor. Season as necessary and serve.

Sundried tomato tapenade

100 g sundried tomatoes, strained

1 good tsp Dijon mustard

1 good tbsp capers

1 good tbsp pitted green olives

2 cloves garlic, peeled

1 tsp chopped rosemary

Juice of 1 lemon

100 ml olive oil

Pinch sugar

Pulse all the ingredients until fairly smooth. Season as necessary and serve.

Prawns with garlic and feta

Serves 10

100 g butter

8 cloves garlic, peeled and crushed

Good pinch chilli flakes

Olive oil

1 kg frozen prawns

Salt and pepper

Bunch flat leaf parsley, finely chopped

Juice of 2 lemons

200 g feta cheese, finely diced

Inevitably it's going to happen. You casually ask someone around for a drink and then, bam, end up in a blind panic about what to serve, as you know that pack of dry-roasted peanuts just won't do. It's always good to have a couple of ideas on nifty nibbles that could potentially be whipped up from store and freezer ingredients. These prawns are perfect for such occasions.

It's up to you how you want to serve them. Either as individual prawns with some of the feta cheese and garlic butter drizzled on top, or, as suggested here, pop them on some bread for a kind of really grubby and delicious open posh prawns on toast! Use whatever prawns are handy: frozen, cooked or uncooked.

You might need to do this in two batches, depending on the size of your frying pan. But regardless, have a big platter or some bits of toast ready.

Melt half or all of the butter and add the garlic, the chilli and a splash of olive oil. When hot (but don't let the garlic burn) add the prawns and turn up the heat. Cook them out, tossing regularly so they are well coated in butter and garlic. Season with plenty of black pepper and just a little salt. Add the chopped parsley, the lemon juice and finally the feta cheese. Mix well. When it's hot through and the prawns are fully cooked, spoon onto the platter or onto toast. Eat immediately.

Prawn/monkfish korma

If you are in the mood to feed a gang, then for ease and flavour, try this recipe. Flicking through Sarah Raven's lovely Food for Friends and Family, her prawn korma caught my eye. This is easy peasy, and the prawns behave impeccably. Any frozen prawns will do, cooked or uncooked. Just cook the raw ones for a bit longer. Serve with your favourite type of rice. If you want to bulk the dish out, add some mushrooms when sweating off the onions, or even some diced aubergine. You can also easily substitute the prawns in this recipe with some meaty white fish, such as monkfish, if it's cut into small chunks.

Serves 4–6

Olive oil

1 large white onion, peeled and finely sliced

3 cloves garlic, peeled and sliced

Good pinch chilli flakes

¼ tsp turmeric

1 tbsp mild curry powder

Handful of button mushrooms (optional), cut in half

1 aubergine (optional), cut into small dice

Salt and pepper

1 (400 ml) tin coconut milk

400–500 g prawns OR monkfish

1 tbsp soft brown sugar

Squeeze of lime juice

Big bunch coriander, chopped

Heat a glug of olive oil in a large heavy-based saucepan and sweat the onion, slowly (about 7 minutes), until soft but not coloured. Turn up the heat, add the spices, mix well and, if using, add the mushrooms and aubergine. Keep the heat high and cook them out; they may go a bit soggy, so keep them on the move to avoid burning, but don't keep at them or they won't dry out. If needed, add another glug of oil, as the aubergine and mushrooms will soak up the fat. Season well and taste them at this stage. If they are tasty and seasoned well, add the coconut milk. If not, keep cooking and season them some more (as well as adding some more spices) until they develop some flavour.

When you're nearly ready to serve, add the prawns (or monkfish), sugar, coriander and lime juice. Let the prawns cook until they change from translucent to pinky orange and are hot through. Bring the curry up to a simmer and check the seasoning. Serve straightaway with rice in a big bowl.

If you want to make this in advance, don't add the prawns or coriander until you're ready to serve. Instead, bring up to the stage of adding the coconut milk, sugar and lime juice and cook for a few minutes, then cool to room temperature and refrigerate overnight. You can reheat gently and then when hot and simmering, add the prawns and coriander. Cook fully and serve.

Oxtail stew

My love affair with oxtail grew from the memory of the delicious but unappreciated home-made oxtail stew that my late father insisted we ate once a week. The best versions, like this one based on a recipe by Skye Gyngell, transform the meat from tough old boots into sticky, gelatinous, fall-off-the bone unctuousness. Yum.

Serves 4–6

1 kg oxtail, cut into thick slices

3 red onions, peeled and sliced

2 tbsp olive oil

Big piece ginger, peeled and chopped

2 red chillies, deseeded and thinly sliced

3 cloves garlic, peeled and sliced

1 tbsp Chinese 5-spice powder

1 litre chicken stock OR vegetable stock

2 x 400 g tins chopped tomatoes

50 ml fish sauce

50 ml soy sauce

3 good tbsp maple syrup OR honey

Put the oxtail in a saucepan and cover with cold water. Bring to the boil, simmer for 15 minutes, then drain and rinse with cold water and set aside on a plate (this cleans it up a bit). Meanwhile, in a heavy-based saucepan, sauté the onions in the oil until starting to colour. Add the ginger, chillies, garlic and Chinese 5-spice powder. Turn up the heat and mix well; the good blast of heat adds colour to the base of your stew and gets the spices working their magic. Lower the heat and add the stock and tomatoes. Mix well, ensuring no patches are starting to burn, and bring to a simmer.

Gently place the oxtail pieces in the sauce, mix well so they are well coated and then cook on a very gentle heat for about 90 minutes with a lid on. Move them about or turn them over every 20 minutes or so, making sure the saucepan isn't burning and that they're coated well and subjected to heat evenly. If the pan is burning, remove the oxtail pieces to a big dish and pour the sauce over them, but don't scrape the pan too well. Just let it drip onto it so that the burnt stuff remains in the saucepan. Wash it well and then put everything back in and keep cooking. You can salvage a stew this way, but it is best to keep monitoring what's going on if you want to avoid this kind of rescue mission.

After 90 minutes, the oxtail should be pretty soft. Add in the fish sauce, soy sauce and maple syrup/honey and mix well. Simmer for another 20 minutes or so. Taste and then leave it to rest for about an hour or overnight. This tastes better when it's had a chance to relax for a bit, and is then reheated to order.

TIP: The end step here adds a lot of oomph, flavour-wise, so I've left out instructions to season with salt and pepper prior to this.

Baked camembert

Serves 12–15

150 g chopped walnuts

2 tbsp soft brown sugar

Good pinch salt

1 kg wheel of camembert

Few sprigs rosemary

1 tbsp honey

Soft, warm, melting cheese, straight out of the oven and just begging to be dipped into with endless crackers and bits of bread, makes this recipe a winner when it comes to impressing friends. It's incredibly simple, but also lip-smackingly tasty too.

If you don't fancy the walnuts, some flaked almonds would also be delicious. If you decide to use them, don't bother dry roasting them first. Just mix with the sugar and salt, sprinkle on the camembert and proceed from there.

Preheat the oven to 180°C.

Put the walnuts and sugar in a non-stick saucepan and heat for a few minutes, being careful to keep shaking them around so that the sugar doesn't start to burn. This will only take a minute or so. Season well and set aside.

Trim the rind from the top of the camembert, as though you were trimming salmon. You just want to remove the top rind; the sides and the bottom need to stay in place.

I bake this in a spring-form cake tin as it is a good fit and easy to transfer onto a chopping board, but you could also wrap it in parchment paper and bake on a baking tray. You just need to be able to transport it once it's hot.

Sprinkle the nuts onto the camembert and stick the sprigs of rosemary into it. Bake for about 20 minutes until it looks gooey but is not an oozing river of cheese. Drizzle a tablespoon of honey onto the cheese and serve with bread and/or crackers. Dig in straightaway.

Fragrant salmon parcels, jasmine rice with spring onion and nigella seeds, and hot and fiery salsa

Sometimes we find ourselves catering for a large group but wanting to do something small and unique, rather than doling out something with a ladle. This exact quandary led me to devise this salmon dish, which, although it comes with jasmine rice, is very accommodating in that the individual salmon parcels look like something Fraulein Maria would consider one of her favourite things. It also has the added advantage of not making your house stink of fish long after you've cooked it, which I find one of the biggest drawbacks to cooking fish at home.

The rice dish may seem a little dull, but it works well, even when reheated the next day, and has a sensible sticky quality and fantastic flavour. The condiment, whilst delicious, is just a serving suggestion and you really do need to doctor it according to your tastes as it can be killer hot.

Serves 4

4 x 200 g skinned pieces of salmon

4–8 basil leaves

4 small bunches coriander

1 lime, sliced

Olive oil

Juice of 1 lime

Salt and pepper

Fragrant salmon parcels

Put each salmon fillet onto a larger rectangle of parchment paper. The salmon pieces I use are long and skinny, so I can sandwich or fold them over, stuffed with a couple of basil leaves, some coriander and a slice of lime. Splash with a few generous drops of olive oil, a bit more lime juice and season well. Wrap up and secure loosely with string. These will be fine for a few hours left in the fridge. Take them out of the fridge about 30 minutes before you are ready to cook, so they get to room temperature.

Place the parcels in a roasting tin. Splash them randomly with some water (about 3 or 4 tablespoons) and bake at about 190°C for about 10 to 15 minutes. I was happy with mine after about 10 minutes, mainly because I liked the fact that they were not fully cooked in the middle. But this is up to you, so open one up, pull it slightly apart and you'll know quite quickly how well done they are. Remember that if they are nearly done, they will keep on cooking in their parcels. Either way, they remain moist so even if you cook them to Timbuktu, they will still be delicious. Let people open up their parcels and empty into a bowl or onto a plate with the rice and the hot and fiery salsa.

Jasmine rice with spring onion and nigella seeds

Olive oil

2 bunches spring onions, finely chopped

2 tsp nigella seeds

3 cloves garlic, peeled and sliced

300 g jasmine rice

600 ml boiled water with a stock cube

Bunch coriander, roughly chopped

Heat up a good splash of olive oil in a heavy-based saucepan (one with a lid) and sweat the spring onions along with the nigella seeds and garlic. Rinse the rice well in a sieve and then add to the saucepan and cook for a few minutes to heat through and also to coat the rice in the oil and flavours. Add the hot stock and bring up to the boil, stirring occasionally. Put a lid on the pan and turn the heat down low. It should cook in about 15 or so minutes, but keep an eye on it, giving it the occasional stir. Check the seasoning. Garnish with coriander before serving.

This dish also reheats very well if you add a bit of water and maybe a splash more olive oil.

Hot and fiery salsa

Few red chillies, seeds removed

3 cloves garlic

Big bunch mint

Big bunch coriander

Bunch basil

Juice of 2 limes

50 ml fish sauce

50 ml soy sauce

50 ml sweet red chilli sauce

1 fennel, grated

Some minced ginger

Salt and pepper

In a food processor, process the chillies, garlic, mint, coriander, basil, lime juice, fish sauce, soy sauce and chilli sauce. Add some water if the mixture is too thick. Taste and add the fennel, which bulks it out and gives it another flavour, along with some minced ginger. Adjust seasoning to suit your tolerance for heat and saltiness.

The salsa can be made in advance as it will keep for a few days in the fridge.

'Six Nations' lamb stew

Serves 12

3 kg diced lamb

Olive oil

Salt and pepper

6 red onions, finely sliced

3 tsp Chinese 5-spice powder

1 big piece ginger, peeled and grated

1 head garlic, peeled and sliced

Good squeeze harissa paste (optional)

1.5 litres stock

4 x 400 g tins tomatoes

4 bay leaves

400 g stoned prunes

50 ml soy sauce

50 ml maple syrup

This is a robust, unctuous stew that appeals to all ages. I regularly make this stew for a large party of rugby fans, who sit on my couch, demanding grub while gawping at the telly. Do try to make it the day before and reheat the next day as it makes life a whole lot easier.

In a large frying pan, fry the lamb in batches in olive oil, season well and set aside. Meanwhile, in another heavy-based saucepan (or two; I use two as I don't have one big enough), sweat the onions in some olive oil until soft. Add the 5-spice powder, ginger, garlic and harissa to the onions and mix well. Cook out for another few minutes. When the lamb is all done, add to the saucepan and mix well. Deglaze the frying pan with some stock and then pour it into the saucepan.

Add the tinned tomatoes and bay leaves along with the rest of the stock. Mix well and bring up to the boil, then simmer for about 90 minutes. I keep the lid on, but after about an hour, remove it so that the stew can reduce and thicken up. Stir occasionally and then add the prunes, soy sauce and maple syrup. Cook for another 20 minutes and then cool slightly and taste. Adjust the seasoning as necessary. This tastes really great the next day.

Roast herb potatoes

Serves 6

1 kg small potatoes

1 red onion, peeled and sliced

6 cloves garlic, peeled

4 big sprigs rosemary

6 sprigs sage

6 sprigs thyme

120 ml white wine

100 ml olive oil

Salt and pepper

2 tsp fennel seeds

This recipe is a simplified version of one in the *River Café Classic Italian Cookbook* and may be my new favourite spudato dish. Chuck in as many herbs as you can and don't forget the fennel seeds, which give it an amazing flavour when baked with the olive oil and wine. They end up almost like crumbly bits of roast potato crossed with sautéed potato, and they are oh so easy to make.

Cut each potato (unpeeled) into 2 or 3 relatively thin slices (about 5 mm thick) and chuck into a large roasting tin. Add all the other ingredients and using your hands – or cheffy wrist action – toss very well so everything gets well coated and mixed. Cover with tinfoil and bake at 150°C (to keep things simple) for about 30 minutes. Halfway through you may flip them over and move them about to stop them sticking and to ensure the wine and olive oil mixture keeps coating the spuds. After 30 minutes, remove the tinfoil and, using a masher, lightly crush or 'squish' the spuds. You don't want to mash them; just smash them up a bit. Add more salt, pepper and some extra olive oil. Toss them around a bit more, then turn the oven up to 180°C and bake for another 20 minutes until tender and starting to crisp. Yum.

Trout and leek pies

Serves 4

375 g puff pastry

Big knob butter

900 g leeks, very finely sliced

1 clove garlic, peeled and crushed

Few sprigs thyme

1 good tbsp anchovy sauce

100 ml cream

4 fillets of trout OR salmon, skinless, 125 g each

2 egg yolks

Small bunch tarragon and lemon juice to serve (optional)

This is a lovely trout-based dish that is special enough to be that once-a-week oily fish dish (salmon would be equally delicious). The recipe was tweaked from an Antony Worrall Thompson one and I think the secret is the anchovy sauce – if you can't find it in a store, mush up one or two tinned anchovies instead. Remember: when it comes to anchovies, less really is more.

Cut the pastry into four rectangles and roll out each one; you don't want it so thin that it can't be manhandled, but it needs to be thin enough to be folded over on itself without ripping. Flour lightly if it starts to stick. Put them on parchment paper and leave to rest in the fridge while you get the filling sorted.

Melt the butter in a large non-stick frying pan or saucepan and sweat the leeks very gently so they wilt down but don't colour. Add the garlic and thyme. Then add the anchovy sauce and cream and mix really well. Turn up the heat to reduce the amount of liquid and create quite a dry mixture going into the pastry. You may wish to season at this stage. When you're ready, roughly chop up the fish and add it to the saucepan. You want the fish to just start to flake, the cream to reduce and for any water coming from the fish to also evaporate. So give it a blast. Mix the fish well (which will become easier as it starts to cook) and then take off the heat and cool down.

You can either chill it right down and make the parcels the following day or else just cool it a little before assembling. If the mixture is too hot, it will make the pastry go all gooey. I can never figure out whether I want to do a crescent shape or triangle, so the parcels can end up a weird hybrid of both shapes. Basically load up one half, leaving a bit of room, with about one-quarter of the mixture. Fold over and press the edges together. Lay the parcels out on a baking tray on parchment paper and brush generously with beaten egg yolks to which you can add a little salt, which will make them looser and easier to brush onto the pastry. Bake at 170°C for about 30 minutes or until golden brown. Cool slightly and serve with some salad and mayonnaise, to which you could add loads of finely chopped tarragon and some lemon juice.

Meatballs with lemon and wine

Serves 6

500 g minced veal OR beef

500 g minced pork

100 g breadcrumbs

1 egg

100 g Parmesan cheese, grated

Salt and lots of black pepper

Few splashes of Worcestershire sauce

Big bunch parsley, finely chopped

3 cloves garlic, peeled and crushed

50 ml cream

2 good pinches grated nutmeg (optional)

To finish:

2 tbsp olive oil, in a bowl

12 thin slices of lemon
4–6 bay leaves

½ bottle white wine

Casual and glamorous, Bocca di Lupo in London, which specialises in regional Italian food, is one of those restaurants that chefs, professional foodies and critics rave about. And who wouldn't champion chef Jacob Kennedy, who says: 'If something can be removed from a recipe and not make the dish worse, I believe doing so will make it more delicious ... I always try to find the simplest way of doing things, so the making and the eating can be as direct and pleasurable as possible. This is the route to happiness.' I couldn't agree more: the way of life referred to – one of simple pleasures – is very appealing.

This meatball recipe is a variation of one of the stars of the *Bocca Cookbook*. The recipe calls for minced veal, which I couldn't get, so used beef instead. But if you can get it, do use it. The meatballs are cooked in a delicious liquid created by half a bottle of wine, some lemon and the fat that comes from the splash of cream, grated Parmesan cheese and minced pork. I love that they need no browning and have a very sophisticated flavour. The aubergine recipe that follows is the perfect accompaniment, being both a lightly pickled salad as well as a sharp, savoury condiment.

Preheat the oven to 220°C, or even 250°C if you can.

Mix all the ingredients for the meatballs together in a large bowl using a spatula. Don't be afraid to season well. Mentally divide the meat in half, and then halve again, so you know roughly how big to make them to yield 18 balls. Have a shallow baking tray ready, possibly non-stick. Press the meatballs between your hands and then dip your fingers into the oil so that your hands become well oiled for the final shaping of the meatballs. Place each one on the baking tray. Continue doing this, using the oil to help stop the meat from sticking to your hands. When you're done, wash your hands well and then bake the meatballs in the really hot oven for about 15 minutes.

Get a smaller gratin dish. When the meatballs are starting to colour, take them out of the oven and turn the oven down to 150°C. Very carefully, transfer the meatballs, turning the underneath side over to be on top. You want them to fit snugly in the gratin dish. Pour any juices from the shallow baking tray on top and then carefully pour in the white wine. Nestle in the bay leaves and top the meatballs with slices of lemon. Bake uncovered for about 90 minutes, basting with the juices whenever you can.

Serve once they have cooled down a little. They need about 5 minutes to rest. They also reheat really well: taking about 20 minutes at 160°C, once they've been brought to room temperature.

Ham hock terrine with celeriac remoulade and salsa verde

Two years ago, I finally made it to the Burren, in County Clare. I felt like some crazed tourist, oohing and aahing at the breathtaking views, and was delighted to find plenty of gorgeous places to eat. One of the best was the Wild Honey Inn in Lisdoonvarna, where chef Aidan McGrath's ham hock terrine was, hands down, the nicest I've ever had: moist, unctuous and not too 'hammy', and perfect with his celeriac remoulade and salsa verde. When I was leaving, I asked for the recipe, and, true to his word, Aidan sent it up for my grubby paws to test.

It really is an absolute winner. Capers, cornichons, parsley, shallots and English mustard all play their part in lifting this keenly priced meat into something light with lots of good flavour. Don't be put off by thinking it's too 'restauranty' to make at home. It really is very simple and it's delicious when devoured with big slices of toast.

Serves 8–10

3 ham hocks

1 onion

2 sticks celery

2 carrots, peeled and chopped in half

Few cloves

2 bay leaves

Few sprigs thyme

Pinch mace

Curly parsley (stalks on)

1–2 tsp English mustard

1 leaf gelatine

Filling:

2 large shallots, very finely chopped

10 small gherkins (cornichons), finely chopped

1 tbsp capers

Bunch flat leaf parsley, roughly chopped

Black pepper

2 celeriac, peeled

Juice of 2 lemons

1 tbsp wholegrain mustard

4 heaped tbsp mayonnaise

Salt and pepper

Bunch basil

Bunch mint

2 bunches flat leaf parsley

1 tbsp Dijon mustard

2 tbsp capers

2 tbsp gherkins

200 ml olive oil

Juice of 1 lemon

Good pinch caster sugar

Salt and pepper

Wild Honey's ham hock terrine

Put the hocks in a large saucepan along with the onion, celery, carrots, cloves, bay leaves, thyme, mace and parsley (but don't fret if you don't have things like mace or cloves) and bring it to the boil. Gently simmer, using a large metal spoon to skim off impurities that bubble up like grey foaming scum. Keep it on a very gentle simmer or those impurities will never have time to settle. The hocks will probably be cooked after 2.5 hours (again, don't worry if you leave them longer as they can take plenty of cooking). Remove from the water and leave in a bowl to cool a bit. Let the ham stock reduce down by about half, as you'll need 300 ml of this to fill the terrine. When the hocks are cool enough to handle, discard the thick skin and some of the fat. But keep some fat and mix it with 2 teaspoons of English mustard. Slide the meat off the bone and keep in a bowl. Measure out 300 ml of reduced stock and allow to cool slightly. Soak the gelatine leaf in some tepid water until it's soft and jelly-like.

Mix the filling ingredients with the shards of ham hock and the fat that's been seasoned with the English mustard. Season with some black pepper. Drop the soft leaf of gelatine into the warm stock and stir until it dissolves. Mix the terrine filling carefully; you don't want to break it up too much. Taste it and adjust the seasoning if necessary. Remember, it will lose some flavour once it has chilled down, so don't be afraid to ramp up the seasoning.

Line a 22 x 12 cm loaf tin with two layers of clingfilm and then pile in the ham hock, but don't press down. Lightly pat or smooth it down. Then pour in the reduced stock. As long as you haven't pressed down the meat, the stock will find the base and slowly fill the voids in the loaf tin. Cover with the overhanging clingfilm and when it has cooled down to room temperature (about 30 minutes), chill overnight.

To serve, use the clingfilm to pull the terrine out of its cosy existence and slice it (a bread knife works best). Serve with toast and the accompaniments below.

Celeriac remoulade

Slice the celeriac very finely into strips, toss it with the lemon juice to help 'cold cook' it and prevent discolouration. Leave to marinate for about 15 minutes. Mix with the rest of the ingredients and adjust seasoning as necessary. This is fine even if made a day in advance.

Salsa verde

Whizz all the ingredients in a food processor, slowly adding the oil. Taste and adjust seasoning. Sometimes, this needs a bit more sugar to help balance the flavours. It will last for a few days in the fridge.

Fried aubergine with mint and vinegar

Serves 4 (side dish)

4 tbsp breadcrumbs

100 ml olive oil

2 cloves garlic, peeled and crushed

Salt and pepper

2 aubergines, sliced 2 cm thick

3 tbsp red wine vinegar

1 tsp caster sugar

Pinch chilli flakes

Small bunch mint

This is a version of another star recipe from the wonderful Bocca di Lupo restaurant in London, which specialises in regional Italian cookery. These aubergines are perfect with the Bocca meatballs (see preceding recipe). They would also be lovely served on a big platter for a casual barbecue accompaniment as they are best at room temperature.

Preheat the oven to 160°C.

Mix the breadcrumbs with about 40 ml of the olive oil and the garlic, salt and pepper. You can always add some dried herbs such as oregano to this or chopped fresh herbs such as thyme and rosemary. Spread the breadcrumbs in a shallow dish and bake until golden brown. You may need to scatter and shake them occasionally as they cook from the outside in. When they feel golden and crunchy, set aside to cool. They are fine to leave sitting out for a few hours.

Heat another 40 ml of olive oil in a large non-stick frying pan and fry the slices of aubergine in batches until golden brown and tanned on both sides. You really need to season the heck out of them. They will just absorb salt and oil. But they will taste fabulous. When ready, lay them out on a platter.

For the dressing, mix the remaining 20 ml of olive oil with the red wine vinegar, sugar and chilli flakes. Finely chop the mint and add it to the dressing, which you can spoon over the aubergines up to an hour before serving. Sprinkle with breadcrumbs and serve.

Crab salad in baby gem parcels

Serves 6–10 (canapés)

Approx. 450 g cooked
crab meat, fresh or frozen

Juice of 1 lemon

Good splash olive oil

3–4 drops Tabasco sauce

1–2 tsp anchovy sauce

2 spring onions, finely
sliced

50–100 ml crème fraîche

Small bunch coriander

Purée:

2 ripe avocados

Juice of 2 limes

Salt and pepper

2 shakes Tabasco sauce

2 packs baby gem lettuce

In summertime, one of my favourite things to cook with is baby gem lettuce. It sounds odd unless you've tried it, but it works a treat, especially with things like peas and bacon. Baby gem seems to be widely available, even in the saddest grocery stores, and is hardy enough to survive in the fridge for days on end.

This recipe is a great bit of party grub. Mixing the crab with crème fraîche and a splash of anchovy sauce (my secret ingredient for mega-umami hits) and Tabasco is really delicious. It is great instead of a 'starter' as friends just grab one along with a napkin and wolf it down. It's also extremely quick and handy as you can easily buy frozen crab meat in fishmongers and supermarkets. Just thaw it out, wash your hands really well and have a little search and rescue for any excess shell. It's not entirely necessary, but even a tiny bit of shell is never that nice to crunch down on.

Pick through the crab meat with very clean hands. Then mix with all the ingredients. Season with plenty of black pepper, but go easy on the salt as the anchovy sauce (and the crab itself) is quite salty. Chill until ready to serve.

Either mash or blend the flesh of the ripe avocados until super smooth with the lime juice, salt, pepper and Tabasco sauce (which you can also leave out of this and/or the crab meat if kids are about or you have sensitive souls).

When ready to serve, cut the stalky bit off the baby gem to separate the leaves. Lay out and spoon some avocado cream onto each one and then top with a generous spoonful of crab. Serve on a big platter with some extra lemon wedges if necessary and a glass of something white and very well chilled.

Cured salmon with avocado and wasabi purée

Serves 4–6

3 large tsp Maldon sea salt

3 tsp caster sugar

Zest of 1 lime, 1 lemon and 1 orange

Lots of black pepper

800 g salmon fillets

Purée:

2 ripe avocados

Juice of 2 limes

1 tsp wasabi paste

Salt and pepper

Sauce:

50 ml soy sauce

1 good tbsp honey

1 good tbsp pickled ginger, finely chopped

Baby leaves

Good sushi is a wonderful thing, but despite how much I love eating it, there's no way I would bound home and declare that, tonight folks, it's sushi for dinner! Yet this version of a recipe for cured salmon from a really gorgeous book, *Bryn's Kitchen*, by Welsh chef Bryn Williams, may well give you the high-voltage sushi fix you crave, without the hassle of making proper sushi.

The only real 'musts' are good, flaky sea salt (Maldon is great) and that you cure the salmon for 8 hours in the fridge. After that, there's not much to it. The avocado purée takes seconds to make and the soy sauce is sweetened – and therefore softened – with some honey. Chopping up the pickled ginger and adding it to the soy sauce, instead of serving it separately, rounds it out even more. The cured salmon really has an excellent flavour, so you just don't want to go overboard on the soy sauce.

Mix together the salt, sugar, zest and pepper and scatter onto a baking tray or gratin dish. The salmon needs to be skinned and pin bones removed. Then you need to chop it into bite-sized pieces. This should leave you with about 600 g of perfect, ready-to-eat, salmon.

Plop the salmon pieces onto the salt and toss until well coated. Wrap the tin or tray really well with clingfilm, so well that you can give the salmon a good shake around the place and scatter and coat without having to open it up, move about with a fork and re-cover with clingfilm. Leave it to cure for about 8 hours.

When you are ready to serve (nearly), rinse off the salmon pieces and pat dry on a tea towel or paper towel – be careful, as the salmon can stick to the paper towel (in which case, just rinse it off and use a clean tea towel). Then chill until ready to plate up.

Purée the avocados with the lime juice and wasabi, and season. Then spread onto a nice platter. Mix the soy sauce with the honey and ginger. Scatter some leaves onto the avocado. Top with the salmon and then drizzle with some soy sauce. Serve on a big platter and let people help themselves.

TIP: To avoid chopping up any salmon yourself, ask your fishmonger to skin it, remove the pin bones and cut it into bite-sized pieces. This means that when you get home, all you have to do is plonk the pieces onto the bed of prepared salt in a roasting tray or gratin dish, toss them around (to get well coated with the salt), wrap the tray in clingfilm and leave it to cure for about 8 hours.

Grilled mackerel with cucumber, chilli and ginger salad

Mackerel is good for you, cheap and oh so fashionable. It works a treat with anything sharp to help combat all its rich, oily goodness. We should be eating more of it. So start with this recipe.

The marinade would do more mackerel if part of a summer feast. If you're feeding just mackerel to guests, then allow one fish (or two fillets) per person; if you want to give only one small fillet per person, then with two fish you'd easily feed four people, hence the vagueness of quantities of mackerel below!

Grilled mackerel

Serves 2–8

100 ml cider OR white wine vinegar

100 ml water

2 tbsp caster sugar

Small bunch coriander

1 red onion, finely sliced

Squeeze lemon juice

2–4 mackerel, filleted and pin boned

Olive oil

Salt and pepper

Heat the vinegar, water and sugar until the sugar has dissolved; then set aside to cool. Chop the stems from the coriander and add them to the vinegar and water mixture. Keep the coriander leaves to add to the cucumber salad (see below). Add the onions and lemon juice. Mix well and then pour this marinade into a shallow dish and marinate the mackerel, flesh side down, for about 20 minutes.

Preheat the grill to its highest setting or do this in one of those fish-grilling contraptions for the barbecue. Score the skin of the mackerel, then pat dry and place on a wire rack, skin side up, and rub with a little olive oil and plenty of salt. Grill until the skin goes lovely and crispy. You won't need to grill on both sides, as the mackerel cooks very quickly. Serve with the cucumber salad.

Cucumber, chilli and ginger salad

50 g caster sugar

50 ml rice wine vinegar

200 ml water

Salt

1 tbsp pickled ginger, finely sliced

1 chilli, deseeded and finely sliced

2 cucumbers, skinned and finely sliced

1 big bunch spring onions, finely sliced

Small bunch coriander leaves (leftover from above)

Heat the sugar, rice vinegar, water and a good pinch of salt in a small saucepan until boiling, then remove from the heat and allow to cool. Add the ginger to the vinegar mixture along with the chilli. If you can't get pickled ginger, just grate a small knob of fresh ginger into the pickling liquid. Mix the cucumber slices with the spring onions and pour over the pickling liquid. Mix well, taste and season. Just before serving, add some chopped coriander.

TIP: I recently picked up a new way of cooking mackerel from Irish chef Richard Gleeson: start with a boned mackerel fillet, skin side down in a non-stick pan with cold olive oil. You need to stay with it and keep pressing it down while you turn on the heat – especially for the first few minutes – to stop it from curling up. Basically, you don't need to flip it over. You just keep it pressed down and when the oil really starts to sizzle and bubble, keep cooking until the flesh goes from beige and pink, to a translucent light beige-grey colour. Once most of the pink hue has gone, it's ready. What you have is a fantastic, even, crispy skin and just-cooked fish.

Mac and cheese

Serves 6

500 g macaroni

Olive oil

Few knobs butter

1 tbsp flour

200 ml white wine

1 tbsp Dijon mustard

Salt and pepper

400–500 ml crème fraîche

4 cloves garlic, peeled and crushed

10–15 smoked streaky bacon rashers, diced

Pinch brown sugar

250 g Gruyère cheese, grated

2 onions, very thinly sliced

100 ml sunflower oil

Over the years, I've been lucky enough to go skiing once or twice despite being pretty rubbish at it. One year in France, whilst mitching from ski school and another inevitable near-death experience on the mountain, I discovered the best reason to go on a skiing holiday: tartiflette – a gorgeous concoction of creamy, bubbling, reblochon cheese, smothering slices of soft potato with bacon, garlic and onion. Alpine gratin potatoes, as it were.

Inspired by this rib-sticking grub, I came up with a macaroni and cheese recipe from a version by one of my food writer crushes, Valentine Warner. His Alpine macaroni was pretty good, but naturally I felt I could tweak it to make it far easier to do for a bunch coming for supper. The recipe easily serves six and all it needs is a good salad, such as the recipe for winter slaw that follows. Hearty appetites and a glass or two of rich, white wine – a Condrieu springs to mind – wouldn't go amiss either.

Cook the macaroni in boiling salted water until nearly cooked (pre-al dente). Drain, rinse in cold water and then pour on a glug of olive oil and mix through to stop the pasta sticking together. Set aside. Meanwhile, take a good knob of butter and, in a non-stick saucepan, cook it with a tablespoon of flour over a medium heat, stirring with a whisk. Cook the roux for a minute or so to cook the flour out and then slowly add the wine, whisking continuously to form a smooth, thick liquid that will look incredibly unappetising. Cook over a gentle heat, add the mustard, season loads and add the crème fraîche and garlic. Cook for a few more minutes and taste.

Heat another knob of butter in a pan and fry the bacon until crisp, adding the sugar to help it caramelise. Drain on kitchen paper and then chuck it into the cream mixture. In a large bowl, mix the macaroni with the cream mixture and the grated Gruyère. Taste and adjust the seasoning. Pour into a large buttered gratin dish. You can leave this overnight and, when ready to cook, heat up for 35 minutes or so in an oven at 170°C until golden and bubbling on top. Cover with tinfoil if the top browns too quickly.

As a garnish, fry the onions in very hot oil until golden and crisp. Drain on kitchen paper, season with salt and sprinkle on top of the macaroni. You're now ready to serve.

Winter slaw with green dressing

Serves 6–8

100 g pumpkin seeds

4 carrots, peeled and grated

200 g baby spinach leaves

1 red onion, thinly sliced

1 red cabbage, thinly sliced

2 Belgian endive, thinly sliced

Green dressing:
25 g parsley

25 g mint

25 g coriander

6 cloves garlic, peeled

Big piece ginger, peeled

Juice of 2 lemons

50 ml soy sauce

100 ml olive oil

3 tbsp honey

50 ml red wine vinegar

This winter slaw does what salad does in summertime: it makes you feel terribly virtuous. The best part of it is the dressing, which is fragrant and fresh and would also be very tasty served over roast lamb.

Prepare the green dressing by whizzing all the dressing ingredients together and seasoning as necessary. This can be used as required. It does lose some of its lovely green colour if you keep it too long in the fridge, so best to make it only a few hours before you need it.

Mix the dry slaw ingredients together in a large bowl and add enough dressing to coat everything well.

TIP: 25 g herbs is one massive handful.

Grilled chorizo with romesco sauce

This is a very handy recipe for nibbles that can be rustled up from pretty regular ingredients that might be lying about in the fridge and store cupboard – perfect for a little canapé with drinks. And, while the romesco sauce might take a little preparation, the grilled bits of chorizo don't need anything except a napkin and a glass of vino.

Grilled chorizo

Serves 4–6

1–2 chorizo sausages

Drizzle olive oil

2 tbsp balsamic vinegar

This couldn't be easier. Slice the chorizo into 1 cm thick slices. Simply heat up the olive oil in a large non-stick frying pan and, when nearly smoking, fry the chorizo over a high heat until it begins to caramelise. A lot of oil will start oozing into the pan. When the slices have got good colour, add the balsamic vinegar and let the chorizo get all glazed up. Remove with a slotted spoon, or just drain on kitchen paper, and serve with some romesco sauce to dunk them into.

Romesco sauce

2 red peppers

2 tomatoes

1 head garlic

60 ml olive oil

Salt and pepper

30 g bread

3 tbsp sweet sherry vinegar

50 g ground almonds

Preheat the oven to 220°C.

Cut the red peppers into big chunks and discard the seeds and stems. Slice the tomatoes in half and cut the garlic head in half, horizontally. Place the peppers, tomatoes and garlic in a roasting tin and drizzle with half the olive oil and season well with salt and pepper. Roast in the oven for 20 minutes until the peppers are just starting to burn.

Remove from the oven, cover with tinfoil and let the steam continue to cook them for another 20 minutes. In a blender, whizz the hunk of bread so that it turns into breadcrumbs and then add the peppers and tomatoes, scoop out the garlic cloves (which won't be that soft) and any juices that are in the roasting tin. Add the vinegar and the rest of the olive oil and whizz until it forms a thick purée. Stir in the ground almonds. Taste and season. If it's too thick, add more vinegar or oil.

This sauce will last a few days in the fridge. Besides chorizo, it is delicious with grilled fish, chargrilled vegetables, frittata or spiced chicken tenders (see next recipe).

Spiced chicken tenders

Serves 4

4–6 skinless chicken breasts

100 g white flour

1 tbsp dried oregano

1 tbsp dried thyme

1 tbsp dried rosemary

Good pinch chilli flakes

2 tsp ground white pepper

1 tbsp sea salt

Loads of black pepper

2 eggs

100 ml milk

250 ml sunflower oil

I've always found it interesting how we can eat larger quantities of certain foods when it's prepared in particular ways. Take fried chicken. There's something about fried chicken goujons or tenders that brings out the greedy white trash in all of us – kids and adults alike.

I shallow fry the chicken for a bit and then finish it off in the oven, which means you can do it for a large group, no bother. It works well for drumsticks, thighs or whole breasts, but I prefer to use skinless breasts, which I serve up as goujons or chicken tenders.

Preheat the oven to 200°C.

If you are making goujons, cut the chicken into strips. Mix all the dry ingredients together and pour into a large plastic bag or small baking tray. Beat the eggs and milk together and drop the chicken into the egg wash and then plop it into the flour and toss around so that it gets lightly coated. Transfer to a plate or baking tray.

Heat up the sunflower oil in a large frying pan. Try to ensure you wash your boards and knives and hands really well after handling raw chicken and use clean tongs when serving up the cooked chicken.

When the oil is hot enough (when you put a bit of chicken in it should bubble away in a very enthusiastic fashion), slowly add more chicken to the pan. You may have to do this in batches. Keep the heat up and when you feel a bit of crust is forming, turn it over so that you get a light golden crust on both sides. This should take a good few minutes. Don't overload the pan or it will become soggy. If the chicken starts burning, turn off the heat.

Transfer the chicken onto a clean baking tray and, when all the strips have been fried, bake it in the oven for another 15 to 20 minutes (longer if using legs or thighs), turning the pieces over occasionally until dark golden brown. Serve straightaway – you can leave them to cool once fully cooked and then reheat in a hot oven for 5 to 10 minutes, but they won't be as crisp.

getting it into them – family favourites

Most people's meals are consumed at home and, therefore, we should be in charge of what's in our fridge and our cupboards.

For me, the rules are simple when eating at home. Aim for at least five portions of fruit and vegetables a day, stay away from highly processed food and drinks, and ensure there is balance. Eating toast and cereal for breakfast, then sandwiches for lunch and pasta for dinner isn't balanced. It's a diet full of convenient carbohydrates. This distorts the fact that carbohydrates , especially ones with fibre, are an important part of what we should be eating – just not at every mealtime. Balance, variety and plenty of raw, fresh fruit and vegetables, wherever possible, is the way to go. We have to eat right most of the time so that we can enjoy our treats and rich food when the occasion calls for it.

Salmon and smoked haddock fishcakes with garlic and herb mayo

 These are very simple and tasty fishcakes based on an Adam Byatt recipe. Although many fishcake recipes use prawns and the like, these ones are free of shellfish, so they're great if you don't like or are allergic to bivalves or crustaceans of any stripe. Also, I know some people hate smoked fish, so feel free to make them all salmon if you prefer.

 You can try one of two cooking methods. Either fry them in oil after dipping in egg, flour and breadcrumbs, and then finish them off in the oven. Alternatively, if you're feeling virtuous, bake them (with no coating) in a really hot oven, on a non-stick baking sheet with a shimmy of oil on it. This 'browns' them on one side and they can then be carefully turned over to finish on the other side. Obviously the coated, fried ones taste better, but if you're being good, or lazy, then do try out the other method.

Salmon and smoked haddock fishcakes

Serves 4–6

400 ml milk

250 g smoked haddock

500 g salmon fillet, skinless

3 Désirée potatoes (approx. 300 g)

Bunch spring onions, finely chopped

Big bunch dill, finely chopped

1 egg, beaten

Salt and pepper

2 tbsp sunflower oil

1 egg, beaten

50 g plain flour

60 g breadcrumbs

Heat up the milk slightly and, when warm, carefully add the smoked haddock, then bring up to a simmer. Add the salmon, bring back up to a simmer and then remove from the heat and set aside.

Meanwhile, peel the spuds, chop into bite-sized chunks and boil in salted water until tender. Drain, and then put the chunks back in the dry saucepan on a very low heat for a minute or so, with a tea towel on top, to help dry them out. Be careful that the tea towel does not go on fire! Mash the spuds with a fork.

Drain the fish and remove any skin or bones and then transfer to a bowl and start to break it up and mash with a fork. Add the spring onions, dill and dried-out spuds. Mix well, taste and season. Bind with the egg, then shape into approximately 12 'burgers' and leave to cool. At this stage you could leave them to refrigerate overnight (once they've reached room temperature), covered with clingfilm.

Preheat the oven to 200°C. Have a baking tray ready to go in the oven.

Heat up the sunflower oil in a large frying pan. Have three plates or shallow bowls ready: one of beaten egg, one of flour and one of breadcrumbs. Dip the fishcakes in egg, flour and then breadcrumbs, and, when the oil is hot, fry them in batches. Make sure they get a good golden brown crust on one side before you turn them over. Do this carefully, but with purpose, so they don't fall apart. When you've good colour on both sides, transfer all of them at the same time to the baking tray and finish cooking in the oven for about 10 minutes. Serve with the herb and garlic mayo.

If you don't want to coat them in breadcrumbs or flour, then heat up a baking tray in the oven with a little pool of oil on it. Then place the fishcakes onto this hot baking tray and bake in the oven for about 10 minutes and then gently turn them over so that both sides get a chance to 'brown'.

Garlic and herb mayo

2 egg yolks

1 whopping tbsp Dijon mustard

200 ml olive oil

200 ml sunflower oil

Juice of 1 lemon

Splash tarragon vinegar

3 cloves garlic, peeled and crushed

Handful chopped dill

1 tsp pink peppercorns, crushed

Salt and pepper

Make sure the egg yolks are at room temperature. With a whisk, mix the egg yolks and mustard. Very slowly add a dribble of oil, intermittently, until you feel it thickening. Once this starts, you can be a bit more relaxed about the pace of adding the oils. Add about 75 per cent of the oils, then mix in the seasonings: lemon juice, vinegar, garlic, dill, peppercorns and salt. Mix well and then continue with the oil until you have the right consistency. Chill until ready to serve.

But! If you can't be bothered with the above, then simply mix the mustard, dill, lemon juice and pink peppercorns into about 500 ml of store-bought mayo.

Hake bake 1

Serves 4

4 tbsp olive oil

1 tsp cumin

1 tbsp coarse ground black pepper

Pinch curry powder

2 tsp nigella seeds

Good few pinches salt

1 tbsp dried mint

200 ml yoghurt

4 hake fillets, skinned

Mint leaves, lemon wedges and olive oil to serve

I'll admit I'm a poor preacher when it comes to the practice of eating fish at home. I think of fish as a luxury, same as meat. But that is ludicrous as many varieties are far cheaper in general and it's much better for you than red meat. If, like me, you seldom cook fish, this hake bake should help change your habits. It's simple and tasty – a perfect midweek dinner – and would also be gorgeous using monkfish, another meaty white fish.

If you're not happy doing it yourself, your fishmonger can remove the skin and pin bone the fish for you. The marinade could be done the night before so that all you need to do is marinate the fish the next morning and then bung it in the oven that evening. The bits of yoghurt seem to crisp and sizzle at the edges and there's usually enough sauce to soak up with a bit of bread.

Heat the olive oil in a pan and sauté the cumin, pepper, curry powder, nigella seeds and salt for a few minutes until you start to get a great roasted smell off the spices. Cool them and add to the mint and yoghurt and mix well. Add the hake and marinate overnight or for only a few minutes – whatever suits. Bake at 200°C for about 10 to 12 minutes until the fish is cooked. Sprinkle with mint leaves and drizzle with more olive oil. Squeeze some lemon juice and enjoy when it has cooled a little.

Serves 4

4 hake fillets, skinned

1 (400 g) tin tomatoes

2 sticks celery, finely chopped

Bunch flat leaf parsley, roughly chopped

1 tbsp capers

1 tbsp caster sugar

Salt and pepper

1 clove garlic, peeled and chopped

Zest of 1 lemon

Olive oil

50–75 g Parmesan cheese, grated

Hake bake 2

This couldn't be simpler. Put the hake fillets into a gratin dish. In a bowl, mix the rest of the ingredients, except for the Parmesan cheese and olive oil. Pour this mixture over the fish and then cover with a generous drizzle of olive oil and a scattering of Parmesan. Bake in the oven for about an hour, at 170°C. Once the sauce has thickened up a bit and the cheese has grilled up nicely, it's ready. Or you could cook it on a slightly higher heat (180°C) for 30 minutes and finish under the grill for about 10 minutes. Whichever is handier.

Tandoori chicken

Serves 6

6 cloves garlic, peeled
and crushed

Big piece ginger, peeled
and finely chopped

2 tbsp olive oil

2 tbsp garam masala

2 tsp ground cumin

Good pinch chilli flakes

500 ml plain yoghurt

2 tsp salt

Juice from 2 limes

6 skinless chicken
breasts

For the dedicated lunch-maker or parent, here is one of those recipes that may give you a little inspiration for creating some exotic delights for the lunch box. But believe me when I say that if my teenage daughter could have her way, her lunch of choice would be white bread with Nutella as opposed to anything below, so don't feel bad if the chicken never makes it into school. You can pick and choose bits that you like: maybe make the chicken tandoori for dinner and use any leftovers to stuff into a pitta bread or wrap for school. While the recipe isn't exactly authentic, it is very handy, and when you're a busy parent – or busy anybody – handy is good.

Sweat the garlic and ginger in the olive oil. After a few minutes, add the spices. Cook for a few minutes to get the flavours going and then turn off the heat and cool down fully before mixing with the yoghurt, salt and lime juice. Slice the chicken into strips and marinate for 10 minutes.

Cook in a hot oven (180°C) for about 10 to 15 minutes, turning halfway through, or better still cook under a hot grill so that the chicken gets charred. You have to turn the pieces over regularly so that they cook evenly. The chicken has a tendency to 'stew' in the oven, so the grill works well or a combination of the two.

Serve for dinner or cool down and refrigerate and use in wraps with avocado, lettuce, tomato and some crunchy chickpeas (see page 79).

Lazy veg lasagne

Serves 8

Olive oil

2 onions, peeled and chopped

6 cloves garlic, peeled and sliced

Salt and pepper

500 g mushrooms, roughly chopped

3 x 400 g tins tomatoes

2 aubergines, diced

10–12 non-precook lasagne sheets

200 ml crème fraîche

250 g Cheddar cheese, grated

I've found a very lazy and vegetarian way of rustling up a lasagne, from start to finish, in just over an hour. It's also one of those dinners that you can get two nights out of, which always makes me incredibly happy. Coming home in the depths of winter and knowing that dinner just needs to be reheated is a glorious feeling.

Initially, I felt the urge to sauté the aubergine separately to get more flavour into it but then I forced myself to cook 'badly' and bung it all in together knowing that if I sautéed it off separately, it would soak up far too many glugs of olive oil. So remember, this is a dish that you hurl together, then layer up and bake. Load up on some herbs or a pinch of chilli – whatever seasoning you like.

Preheat the oven to 190°C.

In a large saucepan, sweat the onions in a good glug of olive oil until soft. Add in the garlic. Season well and then throw in the mushrooms and tomatoes. Together they produce quite a lot of water so when the mixture is bubbling away and very liquid, chuck in the aubergines, which will soak up all that excess liquid. Cook out for about 10 minutes, check the seasoning and even add in some tomato purée and herbs (oregano is good) at this stage.

In a good-sized gratin dish, layer up one layer of tomato mixture, then the lasagne sheets, breaking them to fit, then more tomato, then another layer of sheets and finish up with a very thin layer of tomato sauce. Sprinkle the cheese on top and then dot the crème fraîche in blobs evenly on top of the cheese. Bake at 190°C for 45 minutes until bubbling and golden brown.

Spaghetti with meatballs and tomato sauce

Serves 4

Olive oil

2 onions, peeled and finely diced

6 cloves garlic, peeled and chopped

1 tsp dried oregano

Salt and pepper

250 g sausage meat

200 g minced beef

100 g Parmesan cheese, grated

1 egg, beaten

50 g breadcrumbs

Pinch nutmeg

Sauce:

50 ml olive oil

6 cloves garlic, peeled and sliced

1 bay leaf

1 tsp dried oregano

2 x 400 g tins chopped tomatoes

1 tbsp caster sugar

Splash of red wine

400–600 g spaghetti

Parmesan cheese, parsley and black pepper to serve

When it comes to comfort food, there is definitely something that both kids and grown-ups love about 'spag bol'. Recently, though, I began thinking about something a little lighter and tastier, so spaghetti with meatballs sprang to mind, which seems to be an Italian-American creation rather than anything you'd find in Italy. I find it very hard to think of this dish without immediately casting my mind back to my favourite mob movie, *Goodfellas*, and that great scene where Paulie and Vinnie re-create this dish when behind bars.

I think this recipe is tastier than any Mob creation, thanks to sausage meat, lots of Parmesan cheese, dried oregano and a simple but well-seasoned tomato sauce. Another advantage is that the meatballs can be prepared the day before and fried off just before, and the sauce made the day before and simply reheated then tossed with the cooked spaghetti last minute. I think the only things you need then are a bib, a glass of red and lots of black pepper. Plus a Mob movie, for dessert.

Heat a few glugs of the olive oil in a large frying pan and, very slowly and gently, sweat the onions and garlic until very soft. Then, you need to transfer them to a bowl and let them cool fully before mixing in a food processor (or by hand using lots of elbow grease, or better yet, well-washed hands) with the rest of the ingredients. I use dried oregano, but if you can get fresh stuff, then feel free to chop it finely and substitute one tablespoon of chopped fresh stuff for each teaspoon of dried stuff.

Shape into small golf balls and chill for 10 minutes or overnight. Heat up another few glugs of olive oil, preferably in a non-stick frying pan, and fry the meatballs until dark brown all over (about 10 minutes).

To make the sauce, heat up the olive oil and sweat the garlic along with the bay leaf and oregano. Then add the tinned tomatoes. Season with the sugar, salt and pepper. You could also add a Parmesan rind if you have one spare. Add the red wine and simmer gently for 20 minutes, occasionally stirring to make sure it's not burning because of the sugar. The Parmesan rind can be rinsed and used again or chucked away if it's warbled too much.

Add the meatballs to the hot tomato sauce and heat thoroughly while you cook the spaghetti in a big saucepan of boiling salted water, to which you've added a splash of olive oil. Cook until al dente, drain, add another couple of tablespoons of olive oil and toss. Season the spaghetti and then dish out. Spoon the tomato sauce and meatballs over the top. Garnish with plenty of grated Parmesan cheese, chopped parsley (or not!) and black pepper.

Tomato and wild rice goulash

**Serves 2
(main course) to 4 (side
dish)**

1 tsp olive oil

2 onions, peeled and
diced

Pinch salt

2 x 400 g tins chopped,
peeled tomatoes

2 tsp granulated sugar

50 g wild rice

200 g brown rice

500 ml water

4 cloves garlic, peeled
and crushed

1 tbsp tomato ketchup

1 tbsp Worcestershire
sauce

1 tbsp soy sauce
(optional)

Large bunch parsley OR
basil, finely chopped

4 tomatoes, finely diced

Few of us eat the perfect diet, but I do try to pack in the fruit and veg when possible. This goulash is full of lycopene-rich tomatoes. Lycopene gives tomatoes their gorgeous red colour, but it is also a great antioxidant, helping us to battle nasties such as cancer and heart disease. A culinary no-brainer, then. Omit the soy and Worcestershire sauces to be really good, and add lots of chopped fresh tomatoes and extra herbs. Great for when you get in from school or work and need a tasty snack.

Heat the olive oil in a medium-sized heavy-based saucepan. Add the onions and fry over a medium heat for a good 5 minutes until just starting to brown. Don't let them burn, but do let them start to caramelise. Add the salt, tomatoes and sugar. Cook for another 5 minutes. Meanwhile, put both types of rice into a sieve and rinse well under a cold tap. Allow excess water to drain off, and then add the rice to the tomatoes. Add the water, garlic, ketchup and the Worcestershire and soy sauces.

Bring the rice to the boil, then reduce the heat so the rice is somewhere between simmering and boiling – an active simmer! Leave the lid off, but do stir occasionally to make sure the pan isn't burning. Cook for at least 25 minutes, then put the lid on and turn the heat off. I leave it like this for about 30 minutes. By that stage it will have cooled down sufficiently to make it a good time to taste and adjust the seasoning. Add the herbs and finely diced tomatoes. Either serve or allow to cool fully before covering and storing in the fridge for up to two days. To reheat, either cover with clingfilm and heat in the microwave, or warm up in a saucepan with a little water.

TIP: I like to do double quantities and keep it for a few days – great for when you're short of time.

RDA pasta sauce

Makes 500 g plus a bit extra

4 carrots

2 courgettes

2 sticks celery

8 tomatoes

2 sweet potatoes

2 red onions

2 cloves garlic, peeled and crushed

Bunch parsley, chopped

2 tbsp olive oil

The basic principle here is to chuck it all in, and either use it up within a couple of days, or make a double quantity and freeze some in plastic containers. Even if you end up defrosting the sauce in the microwave, you can at least boil up some penne or spaghetti and, hey presto, you have a super-healthy dinner for everyone.

Peel, wash and chop up the vegetables as roughly as you like. Heat the olive oil in a large saucepan, and chuck everything in. Cook until soft, and then purée in a food processor. Use the sauce straightaway or else cool, transfer into plastic containers and freeze. It's fine in the freezer for a month or two. Simply thaw out and heat in a small saucepan with a little water, and check the seasoning. It is great to do this sauce with no salt – goodness knows we eat far too much.

Pesto

Serves 8–10

100 g basil

6 cloves garlic, peeled

100 g pistachio nuts, shelled

50 g pine nuts

1 tsp caster sugar

Salt and freshly ground black pepper

50 g Parmesan cheese, grated

300 ml olive oil

When it comes to making pesto, you can use any type of nut you like. I like using a combination of pine and pistachio nuts, but walnuts are also good, especially if you are serving it with chicken. This is a great one for kids to make.

Put all the ingredients, except the olive oil, into a food processor and process until the mixture is as smooth as you want it. I prefer to leave it on the chunky side, so tend to process the pesto using the pulse button on my machine. Add as much olive oil as you like, depending on what you are using it for. Continue to process on the pulse mode.

Granola bars

Makes 14–16

45 g pecan nuts

45 g dried apricots, finely chopped

100 g figs, finely chopped

45 g dried sour cherries OR cranberries

30 g ground almonds

45 g pumpkin seeds

30 g sesame seeds

200 g oats

Good pinch cinnamon

100 ml olive oil

4 tbsp honey

75 g demerara sugar

Here's a really good recipe for granola bars that are made with olive oil instead of butter and are wheat-free to boot. If you use agave syrup (instead of honey), then they are also suitable for vegans. Don't worry if you have to substitute one type of nut for another. Try changing the dried fruit also. I don't think it'll make much odds at the end of the day.

Preheat the oven to 140°C. Lightly toast the pecan nuts for 5 to 10 minutes on a baking tray in the oven.

Soak the apricots, figs and cherries/cranberries in a small amount of boiling water for 5 minutes, then drain. Roughly chop the pecan nuts and then mix with the almonds, seeds, oats, cinnamon and chopped fruit.

Heat the olive oil, honey and sugar in a small saucepan until the sugar dissolves, then mix with the fruit and nuts. Mix well. Line a tin with parchment paper (mine is a rectangular tin, that measures 20 cm in one direction). Using a wet spatula, pack the granola mix into the tin and smooth the top. Keep dipping the spatula into some water as this helps smooth it down without sticking. Bake for 25 minutes or until starting to go golden brown. Allow to cool fully, then remove from the tin and cut into bars. Wrap well in clingfilm and freeze, or keep in the fridge.

Parsnip and Cheddar bake

Serves 4–6 (side dish)

1 kg parsnips, peeled

Salt and pepper

2 big knobs butter

200 ml crème fraîche

Good pinch grated nutmeg

200 g Cheddar cheese, grated

I like this bake a lot, and if I were vegetarian I would happily scoff a dish of this on my own. Even better, you can make this ahead of time, as it reheats very well. A good-sized parsnip weighs about 250 g, so four decent-sized ones should do it.

Chop the peeled parsnips into chunks. Cook in salted water until boiling and then simmer until tender. Drain and put back in the saucepan, covered with a tea towel, on a low heat to let them dry out. Then add the butter, crème fraîche, nutmeg and half the cheese. Season well and mash together until soft and well mixed. They will have more texture than, for example, mashed potatoes, but give them a good mash so it looks nice and even. Transfer to a shallow gratin dish and allow to cool. Refrigerate for a day or two until ready to bake. Top with the remaining cheese and bake at 180°C for 30 to 40 minutes until golden brown.

Healing chicken soup

Serves 6 (main course)

1 chicken, giblets removed

Big piece ginger, peeled and sliced into thick chunks

1 large onion, peeled and cut in half

3 carrots, peeled and cut in half

2 heads garlic, peeled and cloves cut in half

Few sprigs thyme

1 bay leaf

2–3 tsp turmeric

Salt and pepper

Few splashes of Worcestershire sauce

A while back at a friend's house for supper, we enjoyed some good old-fashioned chicken soup complete with dumplings. It was a humble dinner that sang with good flavour. A few days later, our youngest succumbed to the ravages of some 24-hour tummy bug, so I made some chicken soup in an effort to tame her tum. It worked a treat, justifying its other name: 'Jewish penicillin'.

This version is dead easy. Rapid boiling for a minute or so is key to help bring to the surface anything that needs to be skimmed. Then, turn it down really low and gently hover around a simmer, or even lower. Quantities are vague, because it depends on the size of your saucepan; as long as the chicken would be comfortably submerged in water (if you held it down), then that's enough. No need to brown bones for this. All you need is a big pot, some vegetables, herbs and a teaspoon of turmeric to give it a gorgeous golden colour.

Fill a big saucepan about halfway with cold water. Carefully add the chicken and then everything else. Always wash your hands well after handling raw chicken. Slowly bring everything to the boil. Turn up the heat and let it bubble away furiously for about 2 minutes. Turn the heat down a bit and use a big metal spoon to skim any scum or impurities from the surface. Turn the heat right down, partly cover the pan with a lid and let it simmer gently for about 2.5 hours.

Carefully remove the chicken into a bowl using tongs. It may fall to pieces at this point, but it doesn't really matter. Continue to gently simmer the soup so that it reduces a little, but do it gently! When the carcass is cool enough to handle, remove and discard the skin. Then set about stripping every scrap of meat from the carcass. Set aside.

Taste the soup to see if it needs longer cooking/reducing or more seasoning. Then drain over a colander and discard the herbs and vegetables. Pour the soup back into a saucepan and either dig in straightaway, chucking in the chicken pieces to warm through just before serving, or chill overnight, so that big globules of fat appear on the surface that you can sweep up with some paper towel.

Lots of black pepper and more thyme, accompanied by buttered Matzo crackers or Carr's crackers, make this a feast fit for kings, or anyone who's feeling poorly.

Blackbean tortillas

Serves 4–6 (snack)

1 (400 g) tin black beans

100 ml crème fraîche

80 g strong Cheddar cheese, grated

1 clove garlic, peeled and crushed

Salt and pepper

4 flour tortillas

Some olive oil

Children wolf these down, but they're also popular with adults. I've found that baking them in a roasting tin works better than frying them. They seem to crisp up better and are easier to flip over. Also, frying stuff means you have to remain focused and pay attention, unlike oven cooking. I kept firing these into the oven, forgetting about them, and then rescuing them and realising they were crisp, brown and delicious rather than burnt and inedible. Always a plus.

If you want to jazz it up for grown-ups, then add a pinch of ground cumin or ground coriander or chilli flakes to the black beans.

Preheat the oven to 200°C.

Drain and rinse the black beans. Mash them to a bit of a lumpy paste with a potato masher. Add the crème fraîche, cheese and garlic, and season well. Mush them up a bit more.

Place a tortilla on an oiled roasting tray and spoon half the mixture into a circle on the tortilla, leaving a good 3 cm rim around the outside. Smooth it down, top with another tortilla and smear or brush the top with some more olive oil.

Bake until it is crisp on the bottom (8 minutes or so). Flip it over and bake for another few minutes, then remove from the oven onto a chopping board. Allow to cool and settle for a moment, before slicing and serving. These are so easy you could just set up a mini conveyor belt and keep churning them out.

Serve on their own or else purée a couple of avocados with some garlic, a splash of Tabasco sauce, a squeeze of lime juice and some salt and pepper for an easy dip.

Crunchy chickpeas

Serves 2–4 (snack)

1 (400 g) tin chickpeas, drained and rinsed

Splash olive oil

Good pinch dried rosemary OR thyme

Good pinch coriander seeds

Good pinch smoked sweet paprika

Good pinch turmeric

Salt and pepper

This is a versatile little recipe that works equally well as a moreish snack or a savoury, spicy filling for a sandwich or wrap for lunch, with avocado, lettuce and tomato thrown in to bulk it out. And if you can get the kids on board with them as a snack, you may even be able to wrangle the crisps away!

Preheat the oven to 220°C.

Toss the chickpeas around a roasting tin with the rest of the ingredients. Get them fully coated in the seasonings and then roast in the oven for 15 minutes or so until golden and crunchy. Serve warm or allow to cool down first (although they do go a bit soggy, but are still very tasty).

Sweet potato wedges

Serves 6–8

4 sweet potatoes

Few tbsp olive oil

Salt and pepper

200 g breadcrumbs

3 tbsp ketjap manis OR hoi sin sauce, let down with some water

50 g Parmesan cheese, very finely grated

2 cloves garlic, peeled and crushed

Few sprigs thyme

Pinch chilli flakes

I stole the idea for these from Yotam Ottolenghi's cookbook, *Plenty*. But he did his with pumpkin and, although they looked fab, I found them a bit awkward to eat. Hence my crafty move to sweet potatoes. You do need some parchment paper and possibly two baking trays. These work very well as a TV snack.

Preheat the oven to 190°C.

Leave the skin on the sweet potatoes and cut them in half, horizontally, then cut each half into 3 wedges. Toss with a bit of olive oil, salt and pepper in a bowl and then transfer to parchment-lined baking trays. Allow them some room to sizzle. Give them a blast in the oven for about 15 minutes while you make the topping.

Mix the breadcrumbs with the rest of the ingredients. Taste them and season. You may need to add some olive oil. They should clump together if you squish them up, but they are a little unmanageable. If they taste good and savoury, then top the sweet potatoes with them. You have to kind of pack it onto each one. Then bake for another 20 minutes or even longer until you have nice colour on them and they are starting to smell good and the sweet potatoes are soft.

Allow to cool for a while and then serve on a big plate.

Cheffy shepherd's pie

Serves 6–8

Few good splashes of olive oil

2 onions, peeled and diced

6 cloves garlic, peeled and chopped

Big knob ginger, peeled and finely chopped

½ tsp ground coriander

½ tsp ground cumin

1 kg mince meat

130 g tomato purée

Good tsp brown sugar

1 stock cube

200 ml water

Good few shakes of Worcestershire sauce

Salt and pepper

250 g frozen peas, cooked

Topping:

500 g potatoes

1 kg parsnips

50 g Parmesan cheese, finely grated

100 g strong Cheddar cheese, finely grated

50 ml cream

Few dots butter

A shepherd's pie is one of those things that people don't really want you to mess with, because it's usually a dish that mum made for us when we were kids, so it holds a special place in our culinary hearts. No fusion fuss or nonsense, in other words. However, with apologies to mums everywhere, this one is very definitely a bit cheffy, but is worth it as it's also very tasty. On those occasions when your home is inundated with family and friends it's a brilliant thing to have ready to go as it easily feeds quite a few hungry mouths and, besides, there's only so much pesto pasta anyone can take (unless you're 12 or under).

To make the meat bit, sweat the onions in the olive oil until soft. Turn up the heat and add the garlic, ginger, coriander and cumin. Let the onions start to brown. Season them just a little. Add the mince and break it up with the spoon and mix it well so the spices and flavours get hold of the meat. Add the tomato purée and brown sugar. Mix well and when it's cooked out, dissolve the stock cube (you may only need half) in the water (which is better if it's hot) and add to the mince along with the Worcestershire sauce. Cook over a moderate heat, let it bubble, simmer and reduce, but give it a stir occasionally. Add the peas.

Meanwhile, get the topping on the go. Peel the spuds and parsnips and cut them into chunks. Cook in boiling water until very tender. Drain and put back in the saucepan over a very low heat with a tea towel on top to absorb the moisture and help keep them warm, then mash. Add the two cheeses and the cream, season very well and mash a bit more.

When the mince is cooked out and very tasty, pour or spoon it into a gratin dish. Use a gratin dish that's 25 x 33 cm. Top with the parsnip topping and dot with butter. Bake straightaway at 180°C for about 30 minutes until bubbling and golden brown.

If you want to do this in advance, let the mince and parsnips cool separately (because they will cool down faster that way) and then layer them up when they hit room temperature. Refrigerate for a couple of days. Bake at 180°C for 40 minutes but be careful it doesn't burn, so you may have to cover the topping with tinfoil.

Hummus

Makes 500 g approx.

1 (400 g) tin chickpeas, drained

2 cloves garlic, peeled and crushed

Juice and zest of 1 lemon

Salt and pepper

Good few splashes of Tabasco sauce

Good tsp tahini

Olive oil

This very speedy (and very low-fat) version of hummus takes just minutes. You can also flavour it with some cumin or more tahini or chilli flakes, or even some chopped herbs such as rosemary. You'll find that making hummus becomes one of those very quick snacks you can whip out and is always a great 'condiment' for kids (and grown-ups) to dunk carrot sticks into, when crisps are beckoning and resolve is floundering.

The whole point of something like this is that carrots, cooked broccoli, celery sticks and even mushrooms can all become a vehicle for something tasty and 'creamy' to eat, which are the textures we like as kids. If you want more crunch, then top with a few crunchy chickpeas. Basically anything goes. Home-made hummus is good for you, good to snack on and takes just minutes to prepare, making it one of the best 'fast' slow foods around.

Just empty a tin of drained chickpeas into a food processor and whizz with the garlic, lemon juice and zest, salt and pepper, Tabasco sauce and tahini. To this, add a few glugs of olive oil, and that's it.

Serve with crudités, or stick it into pitta bread and fill with falafel and a spoonful of Greek yoghurt that has been seasoned with some chopped mint, salt and lots of chopped cucumber.

salads, sides, soups and starters

Some of the recipes in this chapter could also be listed under 'what we eat at home most nights'. A great soup with some good brown bread, a slice of farmhouse cheese and maybe a little green salad is a fantastic supper.

But there are also dishes (like the cheese and thyme potato pots) that are heavenly treats, but too rich for everyday dining. In other words, in this chapter you will find a hodgepodge of mainly vegetarian delights that are good for regular dinners or side dishes, or perfect as a starter to something grander. Dishes such as the mango and coconut rice salad are great to bulk up and send to school or work. So are the soups.

Most of the recipes are also great to have two nights in a row. I often double a recipe to ensure I can get two nights of suppers out of them. Eliminating an hour of prep on a busy weeknight and just having to reheat dinner is always a plus. And anyone who moans 'but we had this for dinner last night' should promptly be handed an apron and invited to take over.

Mango and coconut rice salad

Serves 4–6

100 g jasmine rice

1 tsp butter

Salt

150 g red Camargue rice

1 red pepper, thinly sliced

Bunch mint, finely chopped

Bunch coriander, finely chopped

Bunch spring onions, finely chopped

1 red chilli, deseeded and finely chopped

Zest and juice of 2 lemons

1 medium mango, finely diced

100 g salted peanuts

50 g flaked coconut

Few glugs olive oil

My pal Maisha Lenehan gave me this recipe, which I think she took from Ottolenghi's column in one of the British papers. She says it has converted her to rice salads, which must mean it's good as they're usually deathly dull. Perhaps it's the blend of wild and jasmine rice, or the zing of the mint and lemon, but either way it's a tasty combination of crunch and soft, toothsome rice.

Cook the jasmine rice with the butter and a pinch of salt in 150 ml water until tender. In a separate saucepan, cook the Camargue rice in 300 ml water until tender. Drain both types of rice, rinse under cold water and set aside to cool. Mix with the rest of the ingredients, season well and serve.

Chicory and blood orange salad

Serves 4–6

2 heads chicory

Handful mixed leaves

2 blood oranges,
segmented

3 tbsp olive oil

1 tbsp walnut oil

1 tbsp wholegrain
mustard

1 tbsp tarragon, chopped

1 tbsp mint, chopped

Juice of 1 lemon

Good squeeze honey

Salt and pepper

An assembly of winter ingredients but with a tasty dressing, this chicory and blood orange salad is certainly lively on the tongue. It is just as easily made with some grapefruit if you can't find any blood oranges. Try serving it with some smoked salmon or goat's cheese for a vegetarian starter that everyone can enjoy.

Mix the ingredients for the dressing together, season to taste. Assemble the salad ingredients on plates and drizzle with some dressing.

Cos salad and mustard dressing

Serves 6–8

Bunch tarragon, finely chopped

1–2 heads cos lettuce

Dressing:
1 tbsp wholegrain mustard

1 tbsp white wine vinegar

3 tbsp olive oil

1 tsp caster sugar

100 ml cream

Salt and pepper

Cos is one of my favourite lettuces, with broad, crunchy leaves that are robust enough to take the kind of strong, tasty dressings I love. This cos salad is a perfect accompaniment to the posh chicken Kiev (see page 5) and the dressing would also be lovely with some new season potatoes.

Whisk all the ingredients together for the salad dressing. Mix with the tarragon and toss with some washed cos.

Celeriac and beetroot gratin

Serves 4–6

300 ml cream

Few scrapes of nutmeg

Big knob butter

Salt and pepper

½ head celeriac

1 large beetroot

½ turnip

Although I initially thought this gratin almost too simple to bother with, it has proven its loveliness several times over. It's based on one from Michelin-starred Edinburgh chef Tom Kitchin's book, *From Nature to Plate*. Those wanting a pommes dauphinoise but with more edge will love the earthiness of this. The beetroot turns an otherwise humble gratin into a gorgeous kaleidoscope of root vegetable colour.

But please do remember that it needs lots of seasoning as the flavours are bare to say the least, and you need the salt to bring out the nutmeg and earthiness of the root veg. The recipe makes enough to do a relatively thin layer, but it's very rich and sumptuous so don't panic if you think it's a bit too flat when layering up the vegetables. This would be gorgeous with a roast or even on its own.

Preheat the oven to 150°C.

Bring the cream just to the boil with a few scrapes of nutmeg and lots of salt and pepper. Set aside. Butter a 32 x 24 cm rectangular gratin dish. Peel the vegetables and slice as thinly as you can. I'm not talking newspaper-thin slices here; just slice slowly and carefully. Layer the veg up in the dish whatever way you like and then pour the cream over them. Bake for 90 minutes or until very soft. If it's starting to brown too much, you can cover with tinfoil, but the oven is pretty moderate so it should be okay for that long. Allow it to rest for 10 minutes before slicing and serving.

Lentil, ginger and lemon soup

Serves 4–6

4 tbsp olive oil

4 big carrots, peeled and sliced

½ head celery, sliced

2 red onions, peeled and chopped

Big piece ginger, peeled and finely chopped

6 cloves garlic, peeled and sliced

225 g red lentils

225 g yellow split peas

2 litres vegetable stock

Juice of 2 lemons

Black pepper

Coriander to garnish

I have a fabulous Yankee godmother who is a bona fide health nut and always trying to outdo me in the healthy recipe stakes. She's well aware that I'm partial to red meat, bad fats and sugar from time to time, but I am also quite prepared to lay down the steam gauntlet and not be outdone by this crazed American who thinks the Irish are incapable of cooking without tonnes of butter and cream. This soup got the thumbs up from her, to such an extent that she even asked me for the recipe. High praise indeed.

The soup is bursting with goodness, has no fat (other than a glug of olive oil at the start to get it going) and, once liquidised, has a smooth and creamy texture that is extremely satisfying. Feel free to lash in even more ginger than the recipe calls for as it is one of those fantastic ingredients that does you lots of good.

Heat up the olive oil in a large, heavy pot and sauté the carrots, celery, onions, ginger and garlic for 5 minutes. Rinse the lentils and split peas in a sieve and then add to the vegetables along with the stock. Bring to a simmer and then cook gently for 40 minutes or so until the lentils and split peas are soft. Have a little taste and season. Then whizz with one of those soup guns or use a blender or food processor. Add in the lemon juice and lots of black pepper. At this stage you could also add in some more raw ginger and garlic if you wish. Taste and serve with some coriander and, if required, another glug of olive oil for extra richness.

Roast cauliflower salad

Serves 12

2 heads cauliflower

Olive oil

Salt and pepper

2 tsp mild curry powder

2 red onions, peeled and sliced

Good squeeze honey

50 ml red wine vinegar

100 g golden raisins

2 (400 g) tins chickpeas

Bunch chives, finely chopped

2–3 heads chicory, sliced

100 g black olives (optional), stoned

This cauliflower salad is inspired by a Thomas Keller (of The French Laundry) recipe from his book, *Ad Hoc at Home*. It's nice and casual, but one of those books where most of the ingredients consist of certain vinaigrettes or spice mixes, all of which are another recipe on another page, something I am just too lazy for. So for this recipe I left out a bunch of steps and was entirely happy with the result. Roasting cauliflower is a great way to make it very moreish. Dousing it in olive oil and curry powder and mixing it with a bunch of bitter and sweet ingredients makes it a perfect salad on a day that needs bulk catering.

Preheat the oven to 190°C.

Cut the cauliflower into small florets. Plonk them in a roasting tin. Pour a good glug or three of olive oil over them and sprinkle with seasoning and curry powder. Dig in and scoop them around so that they get evenly coated in the spiced olive oil and are seasoned well. Roast for about 20 minutes until tender and starting to brown (this may take longer). But taste them and make sure they are well seasoned.

Marinate the red onions in the honey and the red wine vinegar along with the raisins. Season well. Drain and rinse the chickpeas.

When you are ready to serve, mix all the ingredients together: the cauliflower with the red onions and the chives. Mix well and add the chicory and the olives. Taste and add some more olive oil and seasoning if necessary.

Quinoa salad with lime and coriander

Serves 4

300 g quinoa

2 onions, very finely sliced

6 tbsp olive oil

2 tsp ground cumin

675 ml stock OR water

3 cloves garlic, peeled and crushed

Bunch spring onions, finely chopped

Salt and pepper

1 jar roasted red peppers (or roast and skin about 6 red peppers)

Zest and juice of 3 limes

Bunch coriander, finely chopped

3 tsp oregano

3 tbsp cider vinegar

Good squeeze honey

Nutritionist Susan Jane White got me hooked on quinoa after I was sworn off it for life following a yoga weekend at which every meal seemed to be tasteless quinoa, accompanied by chanting. I've never been so desperate for a burger and a glass of red wine, so it took me a while to forgive this humble grain. But I do love it and prefer it to couscous: better flavour and better for you.

Put the quinoa in a large saucepan and dry roast it for a minute on its own until you can start to smell nuttiness. Remove it to a bowl for a few minutes while you sweat the onions in the olive oil for about 5 minutes until very soft. Add the cumin and mix well. Return the quinoa to the saucepan along with the stock/water and simmer with a lid for about 10 minutes. Then remove the lid and, if there is any excess stock or water, let it 'dry' off. Add the garlic and allow the mixture to cool down.

When ready to serve, add the remaining ingredients, mix well, taste and adjust the seasoning as necessary.

Cannellini bean salad with curly kale, olives and basil

Serves 4

1 pack curly kale (about 8 big leaves)

Olive oil

Salt and pepper

2 x 450 g tins cannellini beans

70 g black, pitted olives, roughly chopped

2 bags baby spinach

Big bunch basil, chopped

Dressing:

1 heaped tbsp Dijon mustard

1 clove garlic, peeled and crushed

1 squirt honey

50 ml red wine vinegar

100 ml olive oil

I make this salad regularly. Part of its appeal is the crispy curly kale, which gives it a great savoury crunch. It reminds me of the 'seaweed' I used to love ordering in Chinese restaurants as a kid. That kale is so good for you is a bonus, and if you get the knack of cooking it using the method below, you will be forever hooked. Mind you, it takes a few attempts to get it right, as the line between crunchy and tasty versus burnt and frazzled can happen very quickly, depending on the ferocity of your oven.

Preheat the oven to 200°C.

Give the curly kale a good rinse, then roughly chop into large bite-sized pieces. Chuck it into a bowl, still damp, pour on a good splash of olive oil and season with plenty of salt and black pepper. Toss well and then spread out on a baking tray. Bake for about 10 minutes, then move it around so that the bits in the middle are moved to the outside of the tray and the crispy bits are moved into the centre.

You need to bake and check and move the kale around for another 5 to 10 minutes, when it will suddenly change from soggy to super crispy, as though it had been deep-fried. If some bits are bordering on burnt, then move them into a bowl while the rest of it cooks. When it sounds crispy, then remove it from the oven and allow it to cool on the baking tray so that it doesn't go soggy. The hard work is done!

Drain and rinse the cannellini beans and throw them into a big salad bowl with the olives. Mix the ingredients for the dressing together in a jar, and pour most of it onto the beans. Add the basil and spinach and gently toss. Add the kale, lightly toss and serve straightaway. The kale will stay crisp for about an hour, so don't toss everything together until the last minute.

Roast cauliflower salad

Quinoa salad with lime and coriander

Cannellini bean salad with curly kale, olives and basil

Cheese and thyme potato pots

Serves 6 generously

1 kg potatoes, peeled and chopped

400 ml cream

100 g butter

Few sprigs thyme

80 g Parmesan cheese

120 g Ardrahan OR Tallegio cheese, cubed

Salt and pepper

The perfect accompaniments for a tasty stew are often boiled spuds and some carrots, but these little pots of devil-worshipping spuds are even better. I have made them with Tallegio but also gave them a go using the Cork cheese Ardrahan, which is widely available in a good selection of supermarkets and delis. Both cheeses are great to cook with. Obviously the amount of fat in these spuds is obscene, but as a real treat, make them and eat only a few bites if you can't handle the guilt. They are perfect with the Umami beef stew (see page 157).

Preheat the oven to 220°C.

Cook the spuds in boiling salted water until tender and then drain and mash very well. Meanwhile, heat the cream and butter with the thyme until just about to boil. Add the cream to the mashed spuds and mix really well with a wooden spoon. It will be very runny. Fold in half the Parmesan cheese and all of the other cheese. Season well and spoon into individual pots or a suitable gratin dish. Top with the remainder of the Parmesan cheese and bake for 15 to 20 minutes until golden brown and bubbling.

Peaches' potato salad

Serves 4 (side dish)

Approx. 750 g new
potatoes

125 ml olive oil

Juice of 1 lemon

1 tbsp Dijon mustard

1 tsp granulated sugar

2 cloves garlic, peeled
and crushed

Salt and pepper

Bunch parsley, roughly
chopped

Bunch dill, roughly
chopped

Bunch spring onions,
finely chopped

2 tbsp capers, chopped

For some reason people put themselves under enormous pressure to cook something 'different' for dinner every night during the week when there's no need. It's fantastic that they're cooking something home-made in the first place, so they should be patting themselves on the back rather than beating their culinary brows! And I know that if you're cooking for men, there's often the all-Irish male roar that a dinner ain't a dinner unless it features meat. In answer to that, remember that spuds are always a winner and this could be served with some smoked fish, which is the best kind of 'ready-meal' if you're obliged to serve up some protein.

This is another delicious recipe from my sister, and, aside from the herbs, you're more than likely to have all the ingredients at home.

Cover the potatoes in cold water, bring to the boil and cook until tender. Drain and roughly chop the potatoes. Whisk together the olive oil, lemon juice, Dijon mustard, sugar and garlic, then season well. Add the herbs, spring onions and capers to the vinaigrette and then pour it onto the warm potatoes. Cool to room temperature and serve.

Stracciatella (egg-drop chicken noodle soup)

Serves 8–10

1 large chicken

Head of garlic, peeled

Few sprigs thyme

Few sprigs rosemary

10 black peppercorns

1 leek, roughly chopped

Salt and pepper

250 g riso pasta OR any small pasta

Olive oil

6 eggs

300 g Parmesan cheese, grated

Big bunch flat leaf parsley, roughly chopped

500 g frozen peas

There are plenty of times when I cook some really boring grub at home, especially if I end up shopping in a grim supermarket where nothing inspires creativity. Such is the curse of modern-day domesticity: there's little room for any inner goddess, but always room for spuds, baked beans and eggs. Occasionally, however, I get it together to make a big pot of this egg-drop soup, known as stracciatella, which can be reheated and doled out for lunch and dinner for three days solid. It's a perfect spring soup: broth-like, nourishing and tasty. I would recommend a free-range or organic bird – you're extracting every last bit of meat from it, so you can justify the extra cost.

Place the chicken in a large stock-pot and cover with water (about 5 litres). Add in the garlic, thyme, rosemary, peppercorns, leek and a good sprinkle of salt and slowly bring to the boil. You will have to regularly slosh out the scum that rises to the surface with a big metal spoon. Once it's simmering, gently cook for 10 minutes and then turn the heat off and leave the chicken to sit in the water and cook for another hour.

Meanwhile, cook the pasta in boiling water until just tender. Drain, rinse in plenty of cold water until cold and then generously pour on some olive oil and set aside in a bowl, giving it a good stir so that it's well coated in olive oil and won't stick. Whisk the eggs with the Parmesan cheese, add the parsley and season really well.

When the chicken has cooked, remove it from the stock and set aside on a plate. Strain the stock or else just scoop out and discard the bits of herbs, leeks and debris. Heat up the stock and slowly simmer for 20 to 30 minutes so that it can reduce by a litre. Remove and discard the skin from the chicken. Tear off and finely chop the flesh. Remove every last scrap and then discard the bones.

When ready to serve, bring the stock to the boil, add the beaten egg mixture and give it a good whisk so that it distributes evenly, and then add the chicken, frozen peas and cooked pasta. Cook for a few minutes and taste, adding salt and pepper if necessary before serving.

Chickpea soup with curry prawns

Serves 4

4 tbsp olive oil

1 onion, peeled and finely chopped

2 garlic cloves, peeled and finely sliced

Salt and pepper

2 x 400 g tins chickpeas, drained

1 litre vegetable OR chicken stock

1 tsp coriander seeds, crushed

200 ml white wine

Juice of 1 lemon

Bunch chives, finely chopped

Curry prawn garnish:
Big knob butter

1 tsp curry powder

8–12 prawns

Salt and pepper

I use tinned chickpeas at home a lot as they really are a gourmet fast food, but, like most commercial kitchens, at work we soak and boil them from scratch. For the soup recipe below, tinned ones really are fine; but if you're making things like falafel or a salad of chickpeas, there's definitely some merit in using dried chickpeas, which admittedly involves some palaver (see tip below). Here you can avoid all the hard labour; all you need is a tin opener and a blender or soup gun to purée. The prawns add a touch of spicy luxury.

In a large saucepan, sweat the olive oil, onions and garlic together until soft. Season well and don't allow to brown. Chuck in the other ingredients (except the chives) and heat through. Simmer gently for 5 minutes and then mix in a blender or with a soup gun until smooth. Return to the saucepan and check the seasoning.

For the prawn garnish, I use cooked frozen tiger prawns, defrosted thoroughly and patted dry. Heat the butter until foaming, add the curry powder and then chuck in the prawns and, keeping the heat up high, toss around until they are well coated and hot. Season with salt and pepper.

Pour the soup into bowls and garnish with curry prawns and chives (or just the chives and an extra swirl of olive oil).

TIP: Dried chickpeas need to be rinsed really well and carefully checked to remove any tiny stones. Soak them overnight in cold water and then drain, rinse and cook in four times as much water. Simmer for 2 or 3 hours until tender. Not adding salt to the water helps to ensure the skins don't toughen during cooking, although salt can be added in the last 20 minutes of cooking time to season them. Rinse well, drain and, when cold and genuinely well drained, mix with your favourite dressings and salad ingredients.

Baby spinach and avocado salad with bacon and almonds

Serves 4

100 g whole, blanched almonds

Salt and pepper

200 g streaky bacon, diced

Olive oil

Pinch soft brown sugar

220 g baby spinach

2 large avocados

Bunch of herbs such as chives, tarragon, basil leaves, chopped

Dressing:

2 tsp Dijon mustard

1 tsp caster sugar

100 ml olive oil

2 tbsp red wine vinegar

1 red onion, peeled and very finely diced

This is for when you want to eat something green but tastier than just a plain old spinach salad, which is a regular feature on American restaurant menus. Over there, they make them into a bit of a feast: sliced mushrooms, hard-boiled eggs, bacon, even blue cheese. Sometimes it can get a bit too much, but this one is a little more simple but still full of flavour and would be an ideal dinner party starter or lovely summer lunch.

First, make the dressing. Whisk the mustard and sugar together and add the olive oil in a steady and slow stream so that it thickens up. Add the vinegar, season and mix in the onion. Set aside until ready to use.

Toast the almonds on a baking tray in the oven at 150°C for 5 to 10 minutes until golden brown. Season them with some salt and pepper. Fry the bacon with a splash of oil and the brown sugar until caramelised and crisp. Drain on kitchen paper. Scoop out the avocado flesh, then toss it with the spinach, bacon, almonds and the dressing. Add in some chopped herbs. Serve straightaway.

Chilled avocado soup

Serves 4–6

4 very ripe avocados

300 ml cold vegetable stock

500 ml plain yoghurt

Few shakes Tabasco sauce

Juice of 4 limes

4 cloves garlic, peeled and crushed

Garnish:

4 tomatoes, finely chopped

1 red onion, peeled and very finely diced

3 sticks celery, very finely sliced

Splash olive oil

Squeeze lime juice

Salt and pepper

This is quite rich but is perfect as a shot of something delicious, and ideal if you don't want to have a starter but still want something to take the edge off everyone's hunger. It also looks incredibly pretty when served in a suitable glass.

Mix the garnish ingredients together and chill until ready to serve.

Blend the soup ingredients in a blender or food processor until silky smooth. Season and chill until ready to serve in glasses or bowls with some of the garnish sprinkled on top.

Courgette fritters with tzatziki

These fritters are perfect if you want a small, light, tasty dish that is hassle-free. They really are fairly handy to whip up, and although I think they would be the most fantastic summer treat to have with a cold beer or crisp glass of wine before a barbecue, they also make a lovely dinner with a big salad and a blob of the quick tzatziki.

Courgette fritters

Serves 4–6

2 courgettes (about 500 g)

Salt and pepper

2 eggs, beaten

200 g feta cheese

2 spring onions, very finely sliced

2 tbsp chopped dill

2 cloves garlic, peeled and crushed

50 g flour

Olive oil

Lemon wedges

Grate the courgettes on your grater (the side with the largest holes), which only takes about 1 minute per courgette, so don't let this task put you off! Put them in a colander, sprinkle with a good few pinches of salt and mix them around with your hands so the salt gets distributed. Let them sit and drain for 10 minutes, then press down to extract more of the juices. When you've done this, transfer the courgettes to a clean tea towel, wrap them up and squeeze tight so that loads more water comes out. You will be surprised at how much the courgettes shrink down to a very large fistful. When you are happy that they are quite dry, plonk them into a bowl and add the beaten egg.

Using a fork, loosen the mixture up with the egg. Then crumble the feta cheese on top and add in the spring onions, dill, garlic and lots of black pepper. Finally, add in the flour. Mix very well, so the feta is very evenly distributed. You can chill it down at this stage and fry later, or else heat up a glug of olive oil in a non-stick frying pan and, taking large forkfuls, fry blobs of the courgettes in the oil (about 6 at a time) until golden brown on both sides (about 2 minutes per side). You may have to adjust the heat or take them off the heat if they are browning too fast. When they have colour on one side, it's easier to flip them over, but do it carefully! When they are cooked, drain on kitchen paper, season lightly and fry off the next batch.

Serve with lemon wedges. If you need to keep them warm, do so in an oven at about 150°C for 10 minutes.

Tzatziki

2 cucumbers

250 ml Greek yoghurt

Splash olive oil

Bunch fresh mint and dill, finely chopped

3 cloves garlic, peeled and crushed

Juice of 1 lemon

Salt and pepper

For the tzatziki, peel the cucumbers, cut them in half (lengthways) and scoop out the seeds with a teaspoon and discard. Then grate on your grater (with the largest holes) and mix with the rest of the ingredients. It keeps in the fridge for a few days and is delicious on everything.

Indonesian veg salad

200 g baby potatoes
(about 5 baby spuds)

4 eggs

½ head cauliflower, cut
into bite-sized florets

Approx. 110 g green
beans, topped and tailed

1 carrot, peeled and thinly
sliced

4 baby gems

1 cucumber, peeled and
thinly sliced

Bunch spring onions,
thinly sliced

Bunch radishes, thinly
sliced

Dressing:

110 g crunchy peanut
butter

3 tbsp sesame oil

1 red chilli, deseeded and
chopped

2 cloves garlic, peeled
and crushed

1 tbsp sweet chilli sauce

1 tbsp soft brown sugar

1 tbsp soy sauce

Juice of 2 limes

It's aggravating when a recipe calls for half a tin of coconut milk or half a tin of tomatoes. What the heck are we supposed to do with the other half? So I do apologise for the fact that this recipe requires half a head of cauliflower. And just in case anyone is tempted to chuck the whole head in: please don't. Cauliflower is best served in moderate quantities, despite having made a bit of a comeback among the Michelin jet-set. The real joy of this recipe is the satay-type dressing, which is worth making on its own.

Make the dressing by whizzing all the ingredients in a food processor. Then let it down with 50 ml water. Set aside. If you need to refrigerate till later, be sure to return to room temperature or add a splash of hot water to loosen it up.

Cook the potatoes in boiling salted water until tender. Drain and cut in half. Bring the eggs to the boil, simmer for 5 minutes, then plunge in cold water, peel and carefully cut in half.

If you can use one large pot of boiling water to blanch all the veg, even better. So chuck the florets in first (they will take 90 seconds), then the green beans (for 60 seconds) and then the carrots (for 30 seconds). Drain the lot, refresh in cold water and leave to dry on a clean tea towel on a baking tray while you get organised.

Separate the baby gem leaves and lay on a platter. Toss the potatoes with the blanched vegetables, the cucumber and enough dressing and layer on top of the baby gem. Top with the hard boiled eggs, spring onions and radishes.

Sautéed spinach or chard with pine nuts, raisins and curry

Serves 2

2 whopping handfuls of spinach AND/OR Swiss chard

Olive oil

4 cloves garlic, peeled and sliced

3 tbsp pine nuts

Handful of raisins

1 tsp mild curry powder

4 eggs (optional), beaten

Salt and pepper

This is a side dish but with some tweaking it can also be one of those mid-week suppers that is cheap to prepare, nutritious and tasty. The iron overload you get with dark green leafy vegetables gives you a burst of nutrition that seems very fortifying, and this spinach dish is uber-tasty. To make a proper dinner out of it, you can chuck in about 4 eggs at the end, which enriches it well and means you can have one bowl of complete goodness for dinner. However, feel free to ditch this option and serve it as a tasty side dish.

Use whatever combination of big leaf spinach and Swiss chard you fancy. I use two whopping handfuls to serve 2 people. Remove stalks that are very 'stalky'. But this is a big, rough rustic dish, so no need to trim too much.

I know it's a pain to do, but the spinach and Swiss chard can be so unmanageable that it's easier to give it a quick dunk in boiling water to tame it down. So wash it well, remove any stalks that you can't bear and roughly chop. Stuff it into a saucepan of boiling salted water. Push it under and you will see it collapse quite quickly. Drain, give it a light rinse and set aside.

Heat a good splash of olive oil in a large saucepan and fry the garlic. Don't let it burn, but do get it to the stage where you get that really garlicky smell. At this stage, add the pine nuts, raisins and curry powder. This will help 'toast' the pine nuts but watch out as they do burn very quickly. Keep them moving about with a wooden spoon, season really well and then add the spinach. Mix well; turn up the heat and sauté. Check the seasoning and, if you like, add the eggs and mix well. The eggs will scramble and you need to really mix well so they cook and are dispersed thoroughly. Season and serve. A knob of butter would also be delicious added to the spinach to enrich it slightly, if you're feeling naughty.

Smoked salmon and beetroot salad

Serves 2 (main course) to 4 (starter)

Approx. 500 g beetroot

2 tbsp olive oil

1 tbsp balsamic vinegar

1 red onion, very finely diced

Salt and pepper

250 ml crème fraîche

2 tbsp horseradish, very finely grated

2 tbsp dill, chopped

Squeeze lemon juice

4 handfuls mixed leaves

Approx. 400 g smoked or hot-smoked salmon

Everyone likes feeling light and lean in the summer months. Or at least trying to. Long evenings and sunny days can curb appetites for sweet and stodgy and have us grabbing handfuls of leaves for salads. But how do we get a salad over the hump of being a side dish to being full-blown dinner-dinner? Yes, that's right, just a big salad and nothing else. I know in my house it can be a tricky one to sell, so salads usually have to contain a bit of protein to make them feel like a proper 'meal'.

This smoked salmon and beetroot salad is an assembly of ingredients, some roasted and cooked, some cold, along with some leaves and dressing, so the work is reasonably minimal. You'll have a good bit of the crème fraîche mixture left over, which is also gorgeous mixed with some spuds as a potato salad.

Roast the beetroot at 180°C, wrapped in tinfoil, for about 30 minutes. Let them cool down in the tinfoil then unwrap, peel, slice and toss with the olive oil, balsamic vinegar, red onion and plenty of salt and pepper. Set aside for about 20 minutes to marinate.

Meanwhile mix the crème fraîche with the horseradish, dill and lemon juice. Season well with salt and pepper.

Arrange the leaves on plates, top with salmon and beetroot. Spoon the juices from the beetroot over the leaves. Add a few blobs of crème fraîche on top and serve.

Broccoli with sesame dipping sauce

Serves 4–6 (side dish)

2 heads broccoli

Toasted sesame seeds to garnish

Dipping sauce:

2 cloves garlic, peeled and crushed

2 tbsp tahini

2 tbsp crunchy peanut butter

1 tbsp honey

4 tbsp olive oil

2 tbsp mirin

Juice of 1 lime

1 piece ginger, peeled and grated

3 tbsp soy sauce

This is another rather virtuous recipe for veg lovers, though the dipping sauce is a little evil. The fact that kids will happily munch through a pile of broccoli florets if they can dip them into something yummy makes it worth making.

Chuck all the ingredients for the dipping sauce into the food processor and whizz until smooth. Taste and adjust the seasoning if necessary. This will last in your fridge for a few days.

Trim the broccoli and chop up into florets. Blanch in boiling water for a couple of minutes until just tender. Drain and serve while still warm, with the sesame seeds sprinkled on top and the dipping sauce on the side.

Alternatively, you could refresh the blanched broccoli in cold water, toss with some olive oil and chargrill it for extra flavour.

Leek and green split pea soup

Serves 6–8

Olive oil

4 large leeks

1 large onion

2 large carrots

2 sticks celery, including the leaves

4 cloves garlic

200 g green split peas

1 vegetable stock cube

Big bunch dill, roughly chopped

This is based on a recipe from the cookbook of one of Dublin's vegetarian restaurants, Cornucopia. I tried bulking this right up and it wasn't as nice, so stick to the quantities given here.

Heat up a good glug of olive oil in a large saucepan. Chop the leeks and use as much of the green part as possible; this is where all the goodness is! Peel and roughly chop the onion and carrots. Chop the celery. Chuck them all into the saucepan and very gently sweat with the lid on. Do this for 5 to 10 minutes, occasionally adding a little splash of water if you think it's starting to burn. You really want to sweat the vegetables as supposed to browning them or getting any colour on them.

Add the garlic, split peas, stock cube and 2 litres of water. Season well and, keeping the lid on, simmer for about 40 minutes until the vegetables and split peas are soft. Blend using a soup gun and then add in the dill and blend again. Taste and adjust the seasoning.

Once cool, this soup is fine to keep in the fridge and reheat as necessary for a few days.

Roast sweet 'n' sour carrots

Serves 4 (side dish)

Small knob butter

Good splash olive oil

750 g carrots, peeled and cut into thick slices

Good squeeze honey

150 ml white wine vinegar

2 cloves garlic, peeled and crushed

Good few sprigs rosemary and thyme

Salt and pepper

These roast carrots are definitely my new favourite way of cooking carrots. They only take about 10 to 15 minutes to cook, and the flavour really is a magnificent sweet and sour that goes beautifully with roast lamb. I absolutely love taking cheap vegetables, such as carrots, parsnips and turnips, and turning them into something really delicious with just the smallest bit of effort. My default position in almost any meal is always to have some salad, but I have to remind myself to eat more seasonally and therefore embrace all things rooted. After making these carrots, we all decided you could happily devour a bowl of them, with nothing else, for dinner.

Put the butter and olive oil in a large saucepan and when the pan is good and hot, add the carrots. Toss them about so they get well coated and begin to colour. Add the honey and cook some more. Then add the white wine vinegar and cook for another minute to let the vinegar reduce. Deglaze the pan with 250 ml water, season well and add the garlic and herbs. Put a lid on the saucepan and cook for 10 minutes. If there's still some liquid in the pan, cook for a final few minutes until the liquid has evaporated and you are left with beautifully glazed and tender carrots.

Rice noodle salad

Serves 2–3 (side dish)

50 g cashew nuts

200 g rice vermicelli noodles

Small bunch radishes, finely sliced

Bunch spring onions, finely sliced

1 cucumber, finely sliced

Bunch coriander, chopped

Dressing:

1 tbsp stem ginger syrup

2 tbsp olive oil

1 tbsp tahini

Juice of 3 limes

3 tbsp soy sauce

This rice noodle salad could quite possibly be a meal in itself if you increase the vegetable quotient by adding some sautéed bok or pak choi. It is handy to make because of its cold water bathing followed by boiling water dipping (proper instructions below). It's based on a recipe from Simon Hopkinson who, unlike me, is not a lazy bones, so his recipe had instructions for making a ginger syrup and sesame paste. No way Simon. 'Twas much easier to strain a bit of stem ginger syrup (from a jar) and use a bit of tahini (from a jar). But thanks all the same.

Toast the cashew nuts in a dry frying pan until just starting to smell good and then crush with the bottom of a mug. Break the noodles into smaller pieces so that they are easier to toss and then soak them in cold water for 30 minutes. Drain and plunge them into boiling water for a few minutes, then drain again and rinse until cold.

Make the dressing by mixing all the dressing ingredients with a whisk. If you can't get tahini, use a tablespoon of sesame oil.

When the noodles are cold, mix with the dressing and then add the rest of the vegetables and herbs.

Roast carrot, feta and orange salad

Serves 2 (main course) to 4 (starter)

2–4 large carrots (approx. 650 g)

1 tsp caraway seeds

1 tsp fennel seeds

1 tsp coriander seeds

Olive oil

Salt and pepper

1 tsp honey OR maple syrup

2 tbsp flaked almonds

2 oranges

1 tbsp Dijon mustard

1 tbsp poppy seeds

4 large handfuls baby spinach

100 g feta OR goat's cheese

I am always a fan of taking a cheap vegetable and putting a bit of thought and care into making it into something really tasty and the star of the show. This is one of those recipes that does exactly that.

Peel, trim and cut the carrots into batons. Carrots really do vary in size. I used 2 large ones that weighed 650 g but, when peeled and trimmed, went down to 400 g of perfectly chopped carrots.

In a roasting tray, mix the carrot batons with the seeds and a few glugs of olive oil, and season with salt, pepper and some honey or maple syrup. Mix well so the carrots are coated with this sticky, spicy glaze. Roast for about 20 minutes at 200°C until the carrots are a little tender and starting to char. Leave them in for longer if necessary.

While the oven is still hot, toast the almonds briefly.

Cut the oranges into segments. Strain them and keep the juice. Whisk the mustard with a little more olive oil and then whisk in the orange juice. Add the poppy seeds. Season well.

Assemble piles of spinach on plates, top with roasted carrots, almonds, crumbled cheese and spoon over a little dressing. This makes a perfect supper with some extra cheese and bread on the side.

vegetarian

The last few weeks of summer, when there's a chill in the air, can bring with them the dream of winter food. It's a bit like the darker clothes that start to adorn shop windows. When I see maxi dresses and sandals being replaced with chunky knits and opaque tights, I breathe a sigh of relief. It means we can eat food better suited to our climate – no more pathetic attempts at barbecuing and having to eat salads in the rain – which is why the following vegetarian recipes may seem a bit more wintry.

Summer vegetables are complete wusses – all they ever need is a little blanch, a light dressing or scattering of something, and they're ready to go. But winter veg need to be baked, boiled and browned before they really light up.

The following recipes are veggie dishes that I cook at home if I am making a bit of an effort. They are also veggie dishes that carnivores love. We all eat too much meat – except vegetarians of course – so making vegetarian dishes that are meaty and satisfying is the best way to lure our hunters into becoming gatherers.

Sweet potato pizzas

**Serves 4 (main course)
to 8 (snack)**

4 sweet potatoes

2 tbsp pine nuts

300 ml crème fraîche

Pinch chilli flakes

3 pizza bases

2 cloves garlic, peeled
and crushed

300 g goat's cheese

3 tbsp runny honey

Few sprigs thyme OR
rosemary

Black pepper

Olive oil

The 'artisan' pizza bases sold now in supermarkets and delis have become a bit of a store cupboard ingredient for me, although they're usually stored in my freezer. Depending on the brand, the pack contains either two or three bases that are ready to top, so all you need to do is to prep the topping for a really delicious slice of something savoury, which tastes great the next day or served at room temperature.

Preheat the oven to 200°C.

Wash the sweet potatoes and bake them whole for 35 to 40 minutes. While the potatoes are cooking, toast the pine nuts in the oven for a minute or two on a baking tray until just golden brown. Beware! They will burn quickly, so stay on duty.

The potatoes should be softish but not fully cooked when you remove them from the oven. Allow them to cool so that their skin will shrink away and you can just peel and squeeze the flesh away from the skin. When they're cool enough to handle, cut into medium/thick slices. Set aside.

Mix the crème fraîche with the chilli flakes and garlic. Spread a thin layer onto each pizza base, then top with the slices of sweet potato and dot with clumps of goat's cheese. Drizzle each pizza with a tablespoon of honey along with some thyme or rosemary and black pepper. Bake for 15 minutes or so until the bases are crispy and the cheese is just starting to go golden brown. Take out of the oven and drizzle with some olive oil. Allow to cool slightly (or fully) before serving.

Parsnip fritters with cider and mushroom sauce

Poor old vegetarians often get a raw deal when it comes to a roast dinner, unless of course they're the chef. It took some digging to find a dish that is suitably 'meaty' and doesn't involve goat's cheese or red peppers, which many vegetarians view as a cop-out if promoted as the vegetarian option. My quest to find something more unusual led me to these parsnip fritters with a rich sauce, courtesy of Dennis Cotter's *Café Paradiso Cookbook*, from the famed vegetarian restaurant in Cork city.

Serves 4

50 g wild rice

Olive oil

1 onion, peeled and chopped

2 cloves garlic, peeled and crushed

1 tsp fennel seeds

Salt and pepper

1 big or 2 small parsnips (approx.200 g)

3 eggs

50 ml milk

2 tbsp yoghurt

100 g flour

¼ tsp nutmeg

1 tsp dried dill

1 tsp Dijon mustard

1 tbsp parsley, chopped

2 tsp baking powder

Sunflower oil

Parsnip fritters

Cook the rice in boiling water until just cooked. Drain and rinse until cold. You should have about 100 g cooked rice. Heat a glug of olive oil in a saucepan and sweat the onions until soft. Add the garlic and fennel seeds and season well. Add the cooked, drained rice, mix well and set aside. Meanwhile, peel and grate the parsnip to yield 120 g grated parsnips and add to the onion mixture. Continue to cook for a few minutes and then set aside. Whisk the eggs with the milk and yoghurt and then add to the flour, whisking until there are no lumps. Add the nutmeg, dill, mustard and parsley. Then add the onion and rice mixture. Mix well and, when ready to fry, add the baking powder.

Heat a few tablespoons of sunflower oil in a non-stick frying pan and spoon blobs of batter into it to make thick, small pancake sizes. Fry in batches until cooked on both sides and then transfer to a baking tray. Either cool them down fully at this stage and reheat later or finish cooking now in a moderate oven (160°C) until hot through. Serve with a good spoonful of the sauce.

Knob butter

200 g button mushrooms, thinly sliced

Salt and pepper

1 tsp thyme leaves

300 ml cider

100 ml cream

Cider and mushroom sauce

Heat the butter and fry the mushrooms until just starting to colour. Season well. Add the thyme and then add the cider and cream and cook over a gentle heat for 5 to 10 minutes until the sauce reduces slightly and is super-tasty. You may also like to chuck in some garlic. This is fine to cool and reheat.

Gruyère and wild mushroom gratin

Serves 6 easily

4 tbsp olive oil

3 red onions, peeled and sliced

Salt and pepper

200 g 'wild' mushrooms, peeled and sliced

275 g Gruyère cheese, grated

Big knob butter

4–6 slices stale white bread

3 eggs, beaten

200 ml milk

300 ml crème fraîche

50 g Parmesan cheese, grated

Lots of food writers grumble about the fact that 'wild mushrooms' is a bit of a false term for what are, in fact, fancier versions of cultivated mushrooms. There is nothing very wild about the mushrooms we buy in vegetable shops; if anything, they should be called 'exotic, but cultivated, not-so-wild, mushrooms'.

When I came across this gratin of 'wild mushrooms', I was sure it was going to end up a bit too watery rather than rich and creamy, as the mushrooms didn't need a huge amount of frying. However, the bread used to soak up the juices does its job beautifully, and although I'm not a huge fan of a sweet bread and butter pudding, this recipe from Annie Bell is a fantastically umami/savoury bread and mushroom pudding. It is perfect as a full-blown supper on its own, but if you're looking to splurge, serve it up alongside a juicy steak.

In half the olive oil, fry the onions until soft and golden. Season and transfer to a bowl. Sauté the mushrooms in the rest of the olive oil until just soft, and season. Use shiitake, Portobello, brown, oyster mushrooms – whatever you can get. Mix in with the onions and grated Gruyère and set aside.

Butter the bread generously and slice in half into triangles. Line the bottom of a gratin dish with the bread. I use a 30 x 22 cm Pyrex dish. Scatter the mushroom mix on top. Whisk the eggs, milk and crème fraîche together, season and pour on top of the mushrooms. Sprinkle with Parmesan cheese and leave to rest for about an hour if you can so that the bread can soak up the liquid.

Preheat the oven to 180°C. Then bake the dish for at least 35 minutes or so until bubbling and golden. Leave to rest for 10 minutes before serving up.

Roasted winter vegetables with dressing

Serves 4–6

1 red onion, peeled

1 sweet potato

2 carrots, peeled

2 parsnips, peeled

1 celeriac, peeled

2 beetroots, peeled

100 ml olive oil

Salt and pepper

Handful walnuts, chopped

Approx. 100 g feta cheese (optional)

Dressing:

2 tbsp olive oil

Bunch flat-leaf parsley, roughly chopped

1 tbsp balsamic vinegar

1 tsp Dijon mustard

Squeeze honey

Juice of 1 lemon

This roasted winter vegetable dish is rather modest yet tasty, and is certainly a good way to use up those root veg we can all be a little reluctant about cooking.

Preheat the oven to 220°C.

Chop all the vegetables into similar-sized big chunks and chuck into a large bowl. It's okay to leave the skin on the sweet potato. Mix with the olive oil and season well. Move the vegetables to a roasting tin and bake for 30 minutes or so, giving the pan a shake every now and then. Throw the walnuts in for the last few minutes of roasting, so they get some flavour. When the veg are soft and starting to caramelise at the edges, they are done.

Mix all the ingredients for the dressing together and pour on top of the vegetables. Serve while still warm with some feta cheese crumbled on top.

Caramelised garlic tart with goat's cheese

Serves 4–6

500 g puff pastry

3 heads garlic, peeled

2 tbsp olive oil

2 tbsp balsamic vinegar

220 ml water

1 tbsp caster sugar

1 tbsp chopped herbs such as rosemary and thyme

Salt and pepper

120 g soft goat's cheese

120 g hard goat's cheese

3 eggs

200 ml crème fraîche

This version of an Ottolenghi tart recipe is really lovely. It definitely wouldn't be one of my midweek family suppers, but is a must for when you want to enjoy and eat something vegetarian and delicious and you have an hour or two to enjoy making and cooking it.

Preheat the oven to 180°C.

Roll out the puff pastry so that it lines the base and sides of a 28 cm tart tin. If you have the time, stick it in the fridge for 20 minutes or so to rest. Then prick the base with a fork and line the pastry with greaseproof paper and dried beans or rice. Blind bake for 25 minutes, then carefully remove the paper and beans and put back in the oven for another 5 minutes so that the base dries out. Set aside to cool.

Sweat the whole garlic cloves in the olive oil, over a very gentle heat, for 10 minutes. Don't allow them to colour. Then turn up the heat and add the balsamic vinegar, water and sugar. Simmer gently for 10 minutes. Add the herbs and season with salt and pepper. Most of the liquid needs to evaporate and the cloves should be well coated in a dark caramel-type thick glaze. Set aside.

Roughly chop and scatter the cheeses onto the base of the pastry. Use any type of goat's cheese but using some hard and some soft gives a great balance of textures. Then scatter the garlic cloves and any of the balsamic juices on top, arranging the cloves so they are evenly distributed. Whisk the eggs with the crème fraîche and pour on top.

Bake the tart on a baking tray (so that it's easier to transport) at 160°C for about 35 minutes or so until the mixture looks as though it has just set – there's not that much liquid in this recipe so it does cook quickly. Allow to cool slightly before slicing and serving with a big salad.

Falafel

Makes 35

500 g dried chickpeas

100 g flat leaf parsley, chopped

100 g coriander, chopped

6 cloves garlic, peeled and crushed

Olive oil

Salt and pepper

Few tbsp plain flour

Sunflower oil

There was a time when I wasn't bothered making falafel at home, but all that changed with this recipe. It is really delicious, perfect with tzatziki (see page 109) or stuffed into some pitta bread with hummus, lots of salad leaves, chopped tomatoes, a little sliced raw red onion and a good splash of olive oil, lemon juice, salt and pepper. The recipe makes about 35 small balls, but they keep well for a few days, making them perfect for lunch or a snack.

You do need dried chickpeas for this because the tinned ones are just too wet. But the dried ones only need an overnight soak and then they get ground up into falafel, with no pre-cooking.

Feel free to add in some spices such as cumin or ground coriander or even some chilli flakes.

Soak the chickpeas overnight in salted water. Drain, rinse and then blend in a food processor until they resemble fine ground sawdust. Put the chickpeas in a bowl. Process the herbs with a few glugs of the olive oil and crushed garlic. When it resembles green sludge, mix with the chickpeas. The chickpeas should take on a nice green colour. Season well and add enough flour so that when you make a ball between your fingers, it will just stay together. They won't stay together as well as small meatballs will, but they should be strong enough to be shaped and then put on a plate, albeit carefully.

Heat up some sunflower oil and cook off a batch of balls at a time, carefully turning them over when they are crisp and golden brown on one side. They don't need too long to cook. Basically, once they are golden brown on both sides, they are done. Drain on kitchen paper, season with more salt and you can keep them warm in a low oven while you finish the others off. They are lovely cold, and can be reheated the next day, but do taste best when they are fried and eaten soon after.

Spaghetti with no-cook tomato sauce

Serves 2 (main course)

400 g cherry tomatoes

Good pinch sea salt

1 tsp caster sugar

Lots of black pepper

50 ml olive oil

2 cloves garlic, peeled and crushed

1 tsp rosemary leaves, finely chopped

50 g pitted black olives, roughly chopped

Small bunch basil, roughly chopped

1 tbsp red wine vinegar

200 g spaghetti

On a recent holiday we were faced with lovely clean beaches, but some really awful food. The local supermarket was pretty disappointing, so even rustling up dinners became a demoralising affair. Instructed by my family to get over my food grump, I embraced the only available diet of bread, tomatoes and garlic, which we lived on for the week. Luckily, it is a pretty fantastic combination. Each day we sliced and marinated the tomatoes in lots of sea salt with a little sugar and some chopped rosemary and a good splash of olive oil, then we would all fight to get the last few crusts of bread to dunk into the juice to eat.

The tomato sauce below is not dissimilar in concept and makes a fantastic, quick veggie summer supper either as a no-cook pasta sauce or simply as a salad. Easy, tasty and very popular with everyone for dinner.

Cut the tomatoes in half and put them in a good-sized bowl with the salt, sugar, pepper, olive oil, garlic, rosemary, olives, basil and red wine vinegar. Leave it to sit and macerate for anything up to an hour at room temperature. Taste it and adjust the seasoning.

When ready to serve, cook the pasta in plenty of boiling water, drain and toss with a little extra olive oil and season lightly. Mix the sauce with the pasta in the same saucepan and the residual heat will warm it through. Serve immediately.

Aubergine involtini

3 eggs

3 tbsp raisins

4 tbsp red wine vinegar

75 g flour

Salt and pepper

2 large aubergines

300 ml olive oil

250 g ricotta

200 g mozzarella

50 g Parmesan cheese, grated

Tomato sauce:

2 cloves garlic, peeled and crushed

2 x 400 g tins tomatoes

1 tbsp caster sugar

Few sprigs thyme

Salt and pepper

Splash olive oil

As a teenager I spent time working on the east coast of America, where I found that in certain pizzeria joints you could get sandwiches with veal or eggplant 'Parmigiano' – thick, greasy slabs of fried aubergine or veal, with an elasticated sheet of melted mozzarella, drowning in thick tomato sauce. The combination of searing hot cheese, deep-fried aubergine, pockets of burning oil and volcanic tomato sauce – clinging to the roof of your mouth – is not very nice. Greed was an awful incentive for diving in, but wisdom and too many war-stories from burnt, greedy veterans of this all-American fare meant that eventually I came to approach them with a little patience. In hindsight, I'm sure it was pretty awful food, but as a permanently hungry teenager, I was always grateful for them.

These aubergine involtini are much posher versions of the above-mentioned fodder. They take a little time to prepare and are not something I would just rustle up. But the advantage is that once assembled, they are just like a ready-meal in terms of ease of preparation. Bung them in the oven and you're done!

Mix the ricotta with one of the eggs and set aside. Mix the other 2 eggs with a tablespoon of water and set aside. Soak the raisins in the red wine vinegar and set aside. Season the flour with lots of salt and pepper and leave it on a plate.

Slice the aubergine from top to bottom into 1 cm thick slices. Heat up about one-third of the olive oil in a large frying pan and, when hot, dip the aubergine slices into the egg and then the flour and carefully lower into the frying pan. Do this in batches, using the rest of the oil as necessary, and fry until golden brown. Season again when in the frying pan. Drain on kitchen paper while you finish them all off.

Meanwhile, make the tomato sauce simply by simmering the sauce ingredients together and reducing until thick and tasty, which should take about 15 to 20 minutes. Be careful the sugar does not burn. Keep an eye on it and give it the odd stir.

When the aubergines are cool enough to handle, mix together the ricotta with the drained raisins. Cut the mozzarella into thick chips. Spoon a blob of the ricotta mix onto an aubergine slice and add a stick of mozzarella and roll them up. Place them in a gratin dish and either top them with the tomato sauce and Parmesan cheese and bake straightaway or else leave them in the fridge, covered with clingfilm, and when you're ready to cook, spoon the cold tomato sauce over them, sprinkle some Parmesan cheese on top and then bake.

Bake at 170°C for about 25 minutes until golden brown and bubbling. It tastes good to sling some more olive oil on it when it comes out of the oven, along with plenty more black pepper and some chopped flat-leaf parsley.

Puy lentils with sundried tomatoes and Cashel blue cheese

Serves 4–6

500 g puy lentils

Salt and pepper

2 red onions, peeled and very thinly sliced

3 tbsp red wine vinegar

Pinch caster sugar

80 ml olive oil

2 cloves garlic, peeled and crushed

Big bunch coriander, roughly chopped

100 g sundried tomatoes, thinly sliced

100–150 g Cashel OR other soft blue cheese

This recipe is one I now fondly churn out midweek. Please feel free to substitute the blue cheese with a blob of soft Irish goat's cheese (St Tola's would be delicious) or leave it out altogether. A perfect, simple supper. And the lentils are one of your five a day – a bonus.

I use dried sundried tomatoes. If you prefer to use ones in oil, then you need to reduce the olive oil in the recipe slightly and rinse the tomatoes and pat dry with kitchen paper, as they tend to soak up and ooze too much oil.

If you can soak the lentils for 10 minutes, do. Either way, rinse them well and then cook in boiling salted water until tender. This will take anything from 15 to 25 minutes. Meanwhile marinate the red onions with the red wine vinegar, salt, pepper and sugar so that the onions 'cold cook' in the vinegar. When the lentils are cooked, drain, rinse until warm and place in a bowl. Add the olive oil, garlic, coriander and sundried tomatoes, along with the onions, and mix very well. Season and serve in bowls with some blue cheese dotted on top.

TIP: Soaking puy lentils, even for 10 minutes, will speed up cooking time significantly. This is because heat penetrates water faster than it does air, and soaking the lentils helps them to become drenched inside, which means they cook faster than if you start cooking them straight out of the cupboard.

Shakshuka (eggs with tomatoes and peppers)

Serves 2

½ tsp cumin seeds

50 ml olive oil

2 onions, peeled and sliced

3 tsp muscovado sugar

Good pinch smoked paprika

4 peppers (I use 2 red and 2 yellow)

Few sprigs thyme

4–6 large tomatoes, roughly chopped

Splash Tabasco sauce

Salt and pepper

4 eggs

In my quest to make my own version of Ottolenghi's shakshuka, I researched the provenance of this vegetarian dish, with conflicting results. It appears to be from the greater Middle Eastern area, or Tunisia to be exact. Today, however, it has become very much an Israeli dish, at least as far as Israelis are concerned, though if you look closely, each country's variation is in fact almost identical. In one amusing article, Liel Leibovitz of The Jewish Week concludes that shakshuka is perhaps an 'extended metaphor for Israeli society' with its 'multiple origins', it 'immigrated from different countries and cultures, and was infused with foreign influences'. It seems a nice way to describe such a humble dish!

Slow cooking is the key to the delicious red pepper and tomato base. It's fair to say this has become a supper favourite instead of a breakfast one. You could increase the eggs to 6 and serve three people, but have slightly less of the sauce.

In a large, deep, non-stick frying pan (which you have a lid for) dry roast the cumin for a minute or so until you get the best smell. Then add the oil and onions and slowly sweat for about 5 minutes until soft but not coloured. Add the sugar and paprika and stir so that the sugar melts and starts to caramelise. Add in the peppers after a minute, and after another minute or so, add the thyme, tomatoes and Tabasco sauce.

The heat will start to break up the tomatoes. At this stage, put a lid on, turn the heat down low and cook for about 10 minutes, occasionally stirring until it starts to turn into a lovely thick pasta sauce. Taste and season well. You want the mix to taste fantastic! You can either cool it down until the next day or else keep going by cracking the eggs into the mixture and then leaving them to 'poach' on the surface of the tomato sauce. This will take a while, and at times I find myself 'tipping' the pan to get some of the tomato juices to run over the tops of the egg whites to cook them a tad more. Putting a lid on also helps the eggs to cook.

When ready to serve, carefully scoop out so that the eggs stay intact. Delicious with some salad and bread.

Cannellini bean and lettuce soup

Serves 4 (starter)

150 ml olive oil

2 large onions, peeled and very thinly sliced

Salt and pepper

Pinch or two of chilli flakes

4 cloves garlic, peeled and very thinly sliced

2 x 450 g tins cannellini beans, drained

1 litre vegetable stock

4 baby gem lettuce

Juice of 1 lemon

Some fresh basil, roughly torn

Some grated Parmesan cheese

I rave elsewhere in this book about the joys of cooking with baby gem lettuce. I've also sung the praises of that gorgeous London eatery for lovers of Italian food, Bocca di Lupo, whose recipe for cannellini bean and lettuce soup I have tweaked quite a bit to sharpen up the flavours. This is one of those recipes that looks a bit dull initially but springs to life when you cook it.

I don't often think of making soups for a quick supper for fear of all the chopping and peeling, but bar the onions and a few bits of garlic, there's virtually no chopping involved here, except for the very last-minute slicing of the baby gem, which is actually a pleasant task. As usual, I use tinned cannellini beans, and everything else, except the baby gems, are pretty much store-cupboard ingredients, including the whopping amount of olive oil in it, which really makes it taste superb.

In a heavy-based saucepan, heat the olive oil and sweat the onions with a lid on the pan for at least 10 minutes until totally soft and limp. Remove the lid, season them according to the intensity of the stock you're going to add and then add in the chilli flakes and garlic. Move them about and let the garlic and chilli do their magic for another minute or so, but don't let the onions or garlic colour, so keep an eye on the heat.

Give the beans a little rinse while you're draining them. Then chuck them into the saucepan and add the stock. Let this cook for about 5 minutes, bringing to a simmer. Check the seasoning, which should be tasty and broth-like. Then finely slice the baby gem and add it along with the lemon juice. Give it a cursory stir to get it to wilt down slightly, and double check the seasoning before dishing into bowls. Add some basil and a good bit of grated Parmesan cheese. A perfect supper in a bowl.

Leek and bread pudding

Serves 6–8

6 really big leeks

50 g butter

Olive oil

Salt and pepper

3 cloves garlic, peeled and sliced

Few sprigs thyme

1 loaf decent white bread (about 600 g)

500 ml milk

500 ml cream

3 eggs

Pinch nutmeg (optional)

250 g Gruyère OR Cheddar cheese, grated

I love a good veggie dish that works as both a one-pot supper wonder and as part of a Sunday lunch affair instead of spuds, which, while I adore them, I get fed up with every now and then. This leek pudding comes from Thomas Keller of The French Laundry, though in his one he uses brioche, which I replace with a good-quality white loaf. I imagine the brioche cubes would make it even more luscious and rich, but to be honest the plain ones work really well. I highly recommend serving it on its own midweek or as part of something more lavish on a Sunday. It would be gorgeous with roast chicken, I bet.

Preheat the oven to 170°C.

Chop the leeks into 2–3 cm slices and then sweat with the butter and a splash of olive oil in a large saucepan with a lid on it for 10 to 15 minutes until good and soft. Season really generously, and add the garlic and thyme.

While this is cooking, cut the bread into 3 cm cubes and bake in the oven for 10 minutes or so until golden brown. I would also season these lightly. Beat together the milk, cream and eggs. You can grate or add a pinch of nutmeg to this if you like.

When the leeks are good and soft, add the toasted bread cubes, mix well and then spoon into a suitably sized gratin dish. The leeks should come quite high up the dish, but you do need to allow for the cream mixture to go in, so leave enough room. Pour the cream mixture on top and then top with cheese. Leave it for 15 minutes to an hour or so, to soak.

Bake for about an hour until the top is golden brown. Allow to cool a little so the filling can settle, and then serve.

Spaghetti with garlic breadcrumbs and aubergine

Serves 6 easily

Olive oil

4 aubergines, finely diced

Salt and pepper

2 large onions, finely diced

8 cloves garlic, peeled and chopped

2 large tomatoes, roughly chopped

Few sprigs thyme

800 g pasta

Zest of 1 lemon

Breadcrumbs:

3 tbsp olive oil

2 cloves garlic, peeled and crushed

1 tbsp oregano

120 g breadcrumbs

Based on a recipe from a gorgeous book by American chef Laurent Tourondel, this simple aubergine recipe is one of those nice Mediterranean-type dishes that feels very summery. The ragù is delicious on its own, but also as a condiment, with some goat's cheese on toast, or as a side dish with something like roast lamb. If you find caponata and the like too strong, you will like the subtle meatiness of this dish. There are no capers or red peppers to seize the flavours – just lots of aubergine and slow cooking, which produces a summer dish that suits our chilly evenings. Don't feel obliged to make the breadcrumbs. They taste good, but are a pain if you're strapped for time.

Heat at least 3 good tablespoons of oil in a large, non-stick saucepan and fry the aubergine on a high heat in batches and season well. When it's all got colour, set aside and then sweat the onions until soft, in more oil. Simmer the aubergines, onions, garlic and tomatoes, adding a cup of water to help bring it together. Season well, add the thyme and let it cook out for about 30 minutes. It won't look great, but once the water has cooked off and it's cooled down, you should taste great meaty flavours.

Mix all the ingredients for the breadcrumbs together and then bake for 15 to 20 minutes at 150°C until getting brown and toasted. You'll have to mix occasionally and may need to cook it for longer. But do cook them until golden brown.

Cook the pasta in plenty of boiling water. Drain, toss with olive oil, season and add some lemon zest. Mix with the sauce and serve with the breadcrumbs on top.

Paul's Moroccan bean casserole

Serves 8 easily

200 ml sunflower OR rapeseed oil

3 large white onions, peeled and thinly sliced

Salt and pepper

1 large whole piece of ginger

2 heads garlic, peeled

1 tbsp ground cinnamon

1 tbsp ground coriander

2 tbsp ground cumin

3 tbsp mild curry powder

1 tsp chilli flakes

4 x 400 g tins chopped tomatoes

4 tbsp honey

1 orange, peeled and roughly chopped

3 bay leaves

1 (400 g) tin chickpeas

1 (400 g) tin kidney beans

1 (450 g) tin cannellini beans

Squeeze lemon juice

Splash Tabasco sauce

1 tbsp Greek yoghurt

1 preserved lemon

Bunch coriander, chopped

This casserole is from a great young chef called Paul Kavanagh, who also helped cook all the recipes in the book for the photos. It's perfect for late summer. I had to bribe him to part with his trade secrets, and even though his recipe is very simple, in true restaurant fashion there are a few stages you won't feel like doing at home. However, for the very dedicated cooks amongst you – and just to make sure I don't get grief forever more from Paul for altering his beloved recipe – I have given you both options.

Heat the oil in a heavy-based saucepan and sweat the onions until very soft and translucent. This should be done slowly and with a lid on to avoid the onions taking on any colour. Season well. Now Paul's next step is to peel the ginger, roughly chop it and put it in a blender along with all the peeled garlic and 100 ml water. But because I am a lazy wench, I just roughly, but very finely, chopped the garlic and ginger up and added them to the onions. This makes my dish a bit more 'rustic' (read slap-dash), whereas his dish has a much nicer texture. But the flavour is the same.

Once your ginger and garlic are in, keep cooking them out for another few minutes and then add all the spices. Ideally, you need to cook this slowly for about 10 to 15 minutes, which is hard to do without burning the spices. So if you need to add a bit more sunflower oil, do. Keep the heat low, put a lid on every now and then to help keep in the moisture, and keep stirring. The most important thing is not to let the spices burn. When it's ready, add the chopped tomatoes. This will immediately deglaze the pan, so stir well and get everything well combined. Add in the honey, orange and bay leaves. Rinse all the beans under cold water, drain and set aside. Leave the tomato mixture to cook and simmer gently for about an hour, before adding in the beans. Cook for about 10 minutes and check the seasoning. You can sharpen up the flavours with some lemon juice and Tabasco sauce.

Paul makes a preserved lemon purée, which he adds to some natural yoghurt by roughly chopping a jar of preserved lemons into quarters, removing the pips and putting them in a saucepan with 200 g caster sugar and 500 ml water. Cook gently for an hour, then whizz the lemons with about 50 ml of the cooking liquid. Slowly add in about 100 ml olive oil to make a really strong lemon emulsion. He stirs a spoonful of this with some natural yoghurt and adds it at the end. Again, the easy (cheat's) way is to add a spoon of Greek yoghurt and loads of chopped coriander to the casserole and serve with a preserved lemon on the side.

This is a great dish for reheating.

TIP: Paul uses ground spices but was keen to stress the importance of cooking them out – a bit like cooking out the flour when making a roux. If you don't, the end dish will have a very flat taste, so it's important to cook out the spices once they're added to the sweated onions. For those who have a real hodgepodge of ingredients and spices at home, use a combination of whole and ground spices. I prefer to use whole spices, roasting them off in some oil first and then adding the onions to the spices, instead of adding ground spices to sweated onions. But either way, you want to cook the spices out, without burning them, to really accentuate their flavours.

Warm chickpeas with mushrooms, yoghurt and tahini

Serves 4

1 tsp coriander seeds

1 tsp cumin seeds

1 tbsp olive oil

6 large mushrooms, thinly sliced

2 onions, peeled and finely chopped

4 cloves garlic, peeled and sliced

1 (400 g) tin chickpeas, drained and rinsed

1 tbsp tahini

Zest and juice of 1 lemon

Salt and pepper

1–2 tbsp yoghurt

Bunch coriander, roughly chopped

Delicious and deeply satisfying, this is a lovely dish. The tahini, spices and mushrooms give it a wonderful earthiness, which is balanced perfectly by the lemon, yoghurt and coriander.

In a large frying pan, dry roast the coriander and cumin seeds until you really start to get a strong whiff. Add the olive oil, then sauté the mushrooms and onions over a high heat. The mushrooms may exude a lot of water, so don't fret, just turn the heat up and the water will eventually evaporate. The onions should cook down and become nice and soft. Chuck in a knob of butter if you want it richer. Add the garlic, then the chickpeas, tahini and lemon zest and juice. Mix very well and let it cook out for a few minutes. Taste and season well.

When ready to serve, add the yoghurt and give it a quick stir and then pile on some coriander. Serve straightaway.

Pasta with pecorino, lemon and basil

Serves 4–6

500 g pasta

Juice of 2–3 lemons
(approx. 150 ml)

½ tsp caster sugar

300 g pecorino cheese,
finely grated

100 g Parmesan cheese,
finely grated

4 tbsp olive oil

Few cloves garlic, peeled
and crushed

Bunch basil

Salt and pepper

My first visit to the River Café in London was a long time ago but it's a restaurant I always long to go back to. Their recipe for pasta with lemon and pecorino cheese looked too good to turn down, but while they use a combination of fresh and aged pecorino, I could get only regular pecorino, so just used that and didn't fret too much. You could use whatever combo of pecorino and Parmesan cheeses suits. I also added sugar to the lemon juice, as it's a little harsh. Anyway, it is fast, friendly to make and tastes really good.

Cook the pasta in plenty of boiling water. I allow 100 g pasta per person but always have leftovers. Most packs are 500 g, so I did it with 500 g, fed three very generously and had lots left over. It all depends on how greedy you are.

Heat the lemon juice very gently in a saucepan; you're really just warming it through. Add the sugar and stir until dissolved. Gradually add the grated cheese, which will just melt into the lemon juice. It will look a bit like a lumpy roux. Give it some time, stir and heat gently. Then gradually add the olive oil, and keep mixing. Add in the garlic. Then just keep it warm and give the occasional stir.

When the pasta is ready, add a couple of ladles of the pasta water into the cheese sauce, then drain the pasta, add the sauce and mix well. Rip up the basil and mix through it. Check the seasoning, because the pecorino is quite salty, so it's up to you how you need to adjust the seasoning.

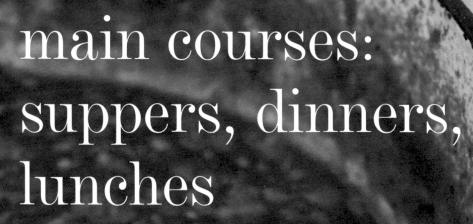

main courses: suppers, dinners, lunches

These dishes are things I cook at home when I have a bit of time to get food on the table: a relaxed Sunday dinner or something I might start the day before. Dishes such as the lamb, beer and black bean chilli or the beef stew with red wine and thyme are things I would happily cook larger amounts of and leave for everyone to eat for a second day.

Although they are all relatively simple, they're not the types of things you feel can be whipped up in a flash. Rather, they are dishes to savour. Relaxed but rich, they remind us of eating really great home-cooked food.

Winter egg supper

Serves 4 (main course)

2 tbsp olive oil

500 g potatoes

1 large onion, peeled and diced

Salt and pepper

100 g chorizo (optional), diced

150 g frozen peas

12 eggs, beaten

150 g Gruyère cheese, grated

100 ml crème fraîche

Watching too much junk TV often makes me think about all those crazy Yankee starlets ordering egg-white omelettes in swish LA restaurants, while secretly craving a doughnut. Egg-white omelettes have to be one of the worst inventions ever. For me, an omelette needs to be yellow, preferably oozing melting cheese, with maybe a sprinkle of mushroom, ham or tomato, and treading the plate with the butter it's been fried in. Certainly not white and bland.

This delicious omelette-type supper dish is a little heavier on the comfort factor than an egg-white omelette and can also be made from next to nowt, ingredients-wise. It ticks all the right boxes: all you need is a fork and a green salad to make it an ideal winter supper. A boring title for sure, but tasty and cheap to beat the band.

Heat up the olive oil, preferably in a large non-stick frying pan or cast-iron pan that can go in the oven. Peel and dice the potatoes; they should be the size of sugar cubes. Let them get a good head start in the frying stakes; they should just be starting to colour before you chuck in the diced onion and continue to cook for 4 or 5 minutes. Season well. Cook for another few minutes as high as you can without burning, but feel free to add another glug of olive oil if this is proving tricky. Add in the chorizo and let it start to caramelise. Taste and when you're happy the spuds are just beginning to lose their rawness, add in the peas and mix together. Take off the heat and add the beaten eggs. Poke around the mixture with a spatula or wooden spoon, making sure the chunky bits are evenly distributed. Then scatter on the grated cheese and spoon blobs of the crème fraîche on top.

Bake at 200°C for about 25 minutes until bubbling and golden but still with the odd puddle of wobble. Let it sit for 10 minutes or so before slicing. Serve with a salad and some warm bread.

Chicken and fennel gratin

Serves 2

50 g butter

50 g flour

Good pinch curry powder

400 ml milk

1 fennel

Olive oil

2 skinless chicken breasts

Salt and pepper

50 g Parmesan cheese, finely grated

There are certain dishes or flavours that when you taste them, hurl you back in time, which is why I spent some time a while back searching for recipes that centred on one of the first sauces I ever mastered: the dear old béchamel (or white sauce, if you're keeping it real).

My former teenage life as an angry vegetarian coincided with my big sister giving in and teaching me how to make béchamel. Needless to say, once mastered, never forgotten or, as in my case, laboured to death. I baked mountains of potatoes, angrily mashing and mixing the flesh with gungy béchamel before re-baking them and foisting them on anyone who looked twice at me. My poor family soon developed a white sauce phobia.

Béchamel has long since been overlooked in favour of emulsions, vinaigrettes and flavoured oils, but now and again you'll see a sensible chef sticking it on a certain dish for good reason. If it's tasty and not used to mask shoddy ingredients, then a good béchamel is pretty delicious. Or at least that's the case here. This gratin just cries out to be made the night before, baked for supper and enjoyed in front of the telly – the perfect ready-made meal.

Melt the butter and then add the flour. It will thicken up like some porridgey muck. Cook out for at least a minute, taking care that it doesn't burn. Add the curry powder, cook for another few seconds and then slowly add the milk and allow it to thicken while whisking gently to get rid of lumps. You want a thick sauce, so don't be tempted to let it down with more milk. Season well and allow it to cool, fully.

Cook the fennel in boiling salted water for a few minutes. Drain and rinse until cold and then slice into four rounds. Grease a small gratin dish with olive oil. Put the fennel rounds in the dish and place the chicken breasts on top. Season well and then spoon the cold béchamel on top of the chicken. Don't worry about spreading it out evenly as it will spread itself when you cook it. Top with the Parmesan cheese and refrigerate overnight if you like or bake straightaway in a preheated oven at 190°C for 30 to 40 minutes until golden brown.

Gammon with parsley sauce

Serves 8

Approx. 1.8 kg gammon

1 onion, peeled and quartered

1 carrot, peeled and quartered

1 leek, roughly chopped

2 bay leaves

12 black peppercorns

Few parsley stalks

Parsley sauce:

50 g butter

50 g flour

Approx. 400 ml gammon cooking liquor

250 ml milk

2 big bunches curly parsley

Black pepper

Here is another recipe that makes good use of béchamel. This time it makes a tasty parsley sauce to accompany some boiled ham and spuds. It's an oldie, but a goodie.

Put the gammon in a large saucepan and cover with cold water. If you need to rinse it once and refill, do so. Chuck the other ingredients on top and boil gently for about 45 minutes per kilo. Leave it to cool in the cooking stock for about 30 minutes before removing, trimming the excess fat and slicing. Put the slices on a platter, cover with some cooking liquor and tinfoil and keep warm while you finish the sauce.

To make the sauce, melt the butter and then add the flour. It will thicken up like some porridgey muck. Cook out for at least a minute, taking care that it doesn't burn and then slowly add the hot cooking liquor and then some milk. Alternate between the two and taste the sauce. The cooking liquor will give you flavour and the milk will give you richness. Allow it to thicken while you whisk gently, getting rid of the lumps. Chop up the parsley and add it at the last minute. Season with lots of black pepper.

When the sauce is good and hot, pour over slices of the boiled gammon. Serve straightaway with boiled spuds and carrots.

Beef stew with red wine and thyme

Serves 4–6

1.5 kg beef, suitable for stewing, cut into 1-inch cubes

Olive oil

Salt and pepper

1 large onion, peeled and sliced

3 carrots, peeled and chopped into chunks

½ head celery, finely sliced

4 cloves garlic, peeled and sliced

Bunch fresh thyme, remove stalks and roughly chop leaves

1 (30 g) tin anchovies, drained

1 bottle red wine

Squeeze harissa

Good pinch Chinese 5-spice powder

100 g gnocchi (optional)

100–200 g frozen peas (optional)

As a compulsive cookbook shopper, I often find myself being disappointed with hastily purchased new books and going back to the ones that have been all but forgotten. A classic example is my old copy of Nigella Lawson's first book, *How to Eat*, a reminder that we fell in love with Nigella for a jolly good reason: she is a great writer. And the book is packed with good recipes.

Anyway, I intended to make her beef stew with anchovies and thyme but digressed entirely, eliminating the flour and beef stock. The result was a really unctuous stew. Served with some boiled spuds or, even better, some gnocchi and a squeeze of frozen peas, this makes a very complete and delicious dinner. Don't tell anyone it contains a tin of anchovies; they'll never know and the 'smackiness' of the umami-inducing anchovies gives the stew a savoury edge.

Preheat the oven to 150°C.

I was under severe time constraints when I made this, so I started by frying the beef in batches in a large frying pan in a little olive oil and I seasoned it really well. In the big ovenproof saucepan, with a lid on it, that I was going to cook the stew in, I added a bit of olive oil and, on a decent heat, started frying the onions, then the carrots and celery along with the garlic and thyme. When the beef was brown enough, I transferred it into the saucepan, and heated up the frying pan again with some more oil and browned the rest of the beef. If you need to deglaze the frying pan, then a good splash of water or some of the wine will do. But make sure you pour the juices into the saucepan. Add the anchovies and red wine to the vegetables. Mix well. Add the harissa and the 5-spice powder. Mix really well.

Cook in the oven for at least 2 and preferably 3 hours. Keep the lid on and taste after an hour or so. If you feel it needs some more liquid, add some hot water; if there's too much liquid, leave the lid off for 20 minutes to reduce it. The anchovies are quite salty, so you'll find that it has plenty of flavour.

Just before serving you can add some gnocchi directly to the stew. If it's too dry for them to cook properly, cook them first in a small saucepan for a couple of minutes, drain and add to the stew. You can also add a couple of handfuls of peas and cook until they are hot through. Allow it to relax for a few minutes before serving.

Umami beef stew

Serves 4–6

Olive oil

1.2 kg chuck steak, cut into 2–3 cm chunks

1.5 litres stock OR water

2 onions, peeled and chopped

½ head garlic, peeled and sliced

6–8 smoked streaky rashers, diced

1 (50 g) tin anchovy fillets in oil

2 heaped tbsp tomato purée

2 bay leaves

300 ml wine

Salt and pepper

If you've recently had your food product antennae out, you'll know all about umami – that fifth taste sensation roughly described by scientists as 'deliciousness'. The umami flavour is found in things like Parmesan cheese and meat, where a particularly savoury taste is imparted by a high presence of glutamates (a common amino acid) that occur naturally in such foods.

Keen to create this 'flavour bomb' at home, I set out to make an umami-rich beef stew in about 15 minutes' preparation time and 2 hours' cooking time in the oven. The result? A tasty stew that goes really well with some boiled spuds and carrots or, even better, with the evil pots of cheesy spuds (see page 99).

I use one heavy saucepan and one frying pan simultaneously to save on time. The stew will cook better in the oven in a heavy cast-iron pot like a Le Creuset pan. If using a lighter pan, you may need to cook it for longer at a gentler oven temperature, reduced by 20°C, with cooking time upped by 45 minutes.

In a heavy-based saucepan, heat a few tablespoons of olive oil and cook the steak on a very high heat so it really browns all over – a good 10 minutes. Then add the stock to the meat and let it deglaze the pan (if much fat and scum rise to the surface, scoop it out). Keep the meat simmering gently and get the frying pan going.

In the frying pan, heat up another tablespoon of olive oil and fry the onions until just starting to colour, then add the garlic and diced rashers. Let some of the fat cook off and let the bacon start to brown. Add in the anchovy fillets (including the oil), tomato purée and bay leaves. Mix really well and mush the anchovies with your wooden spoon. Add the wine, which will deglaze the pan. Carefully transfer the hot onion mixture to the beef. Give it a good stir and season with lots of black pepper, but no salt yet.

Place in the oven and cook with a lid on for an hour. Taste, season, take the lid half off and cook for another hour. The stew should be good and thick and very tasty. Season and cook for another 10 to 15 minutes if necessary. Serve with spuds.

Needless to say, this would taste even better if reheated the next day.

Sliced sea bass with soy and shredded vegetables

Serves 2

Approx. 500 g sea bass, filleted

1 tbsp flour

Juice of 1 lemon

2 tbsp soy sauce

5 cm piece fresh ginger, grated

1 clove garlic, peeled and crushed

2 tbsp olive oil

450 g baby spinach

1 carrot, peeled and very thinly sliced

4 spring onions, finely chopped

1 red chilli, deseeded and thinly sliced

50 g butter

London chef Alastair Little was considered by many critics to be the godfather of modern British cooking in the late 1980s and early 1990s. As a self-taught chef with two restaurants, he fell in love with all things Italian and was responsible for many of the culinary afflictions some of us have since grown to hate: including rocket with everything, sundried anything and carpaccio of someone.

I happen to be a big fan, mainly because he remained pretty true to his craft and didn't go down the celebrity chef route with a plethora of TV shows, public spatting and potty language. And 20 years later, it's lovely to go back and flick through his books. Food, like fashion, can be cyclical, but while his food photography might be out of date, his dishes and cooking style aren't. I was delighted with the ease and tastiness of this dish. Although he concedes that the addition of butter isn't very 'Cantonese', he rightly points out that its luxuriousness goes really well with the astringent soy sauce. I couldn't agree more.

Slice the sea bass into diagonal slices and set aside on a plate, ready to dip into the flour. Mix the lemon juice, soy sauce, ginger and garlic together and set aside. In a large frying pan, heat up a tablespoon of olive oil and wilt the spinach. Remove the spinach from the pan and drain on a clean tea towel or some kitchen paper. Wipe the frying pan dry and then heat up the other tablespoon of olive oil. Dip the slices of sea bass into the flour and fry in the hot oil for about a minute and then flip over and turn down the heat. Pour on the soy sauce mixture and add the vegetables and dry spinach as well as the chilli. Gently toss and then add in the butter in small chunks. Give the juices a swirl around the pan, basting the fish. Serve straightaway.

Belgian endive croque monsieur

Serves 4

4 Belgian endives

40 g butter

Salt and pepper

150 g cooked ham, diced

200 ml cream

100 ml stock

2 cloves garlic, peeled and crushed

Few sprigs thyme

150 g Gruyère cheese, grated

When searching for nutritional things to say about Belgian endive, I was stunned to see that this vegetable has its own website, which I thought was kind of vain for a bitter-tasting leaf that many people aren't crazy about. Talk about self-promotion. But it got worse as I read on. It was like the Madonna of vegetables, declaring that genuine Belgian endive 'isn't any one thing. It's everything.'

Now, I may not go as far as that, but I do like slicing up a few leaves into salads for a wintry zing that feels more in keeping with frosty weather. My favourite method of preparation, however, is to fry it in a little butter and olive oil and then braise it, once coloured. In other words, it's good to cook the heck out of it. Hence, this tasty recipe – so tasty that even the child ate a few bites and declared it: 'Okay'.

Preheat the oven to 200°C.

Slice the endive in half (lengthways). Melt the butter in a large frying pan and fry the endive flat side down for a few minutes until starting to brown. Season well and then transfer to a gratin dish. You may need to fry them in two or three batches depending on the size of your frying pan and you may need more butter. Once you've browned off all the endive and have them neatly lined up in the gratin dish, in one single layer rather than piled on top of each other, top them with the ham.

Heat up the cream and stock in the frying pan, add the garlic and thyme leaves. When hot and tasty, pour on top of the endive, top with the cheese and bake for 30 minutes or until golden brown. You may want to baste the endive halfway through cooking.

Serve with some bread and salad for a tasty supper dish.

Spiced chicken with garlic cream

When it comes to fried chicken, I've tested quite a few recipes, and while I try not to make a habit of lecturing people on what ingredients to buy, I would strongly recommend buying a flaky sea salt for this recipe, like Maldon. The recipe calls for one tablespoon of salt, and if you use a fine sea salt instead, you will feel like you've drunk the entire Irish sea. If you can't get Maldon, then reduce the salt drastically to one scant teaspoon.

This recipe is a version of one of the best fried chicken recipes I've found to date. It's by Simon Hopkinson and it is pretty emphatic in the amount of egg and flour dunking and bathing the chicken has to do. Although it may seem arduous, the end result means that the chicken is very crisp and remains so, even when reheated in the oven the next day. The accompanying garlic cream is a bit OTT in terms of the garlic quotient, but is very tasty indeed. Perfect to blob on some baked potatoes.

Spiced chicken
Preheat the oven to 160°C.

Serves 4–6

100 g flour

1 tsp celery salt

1 tsp garlic powder

1 tsp paprika

1 tsp white pepper

1 tbsp Maldon sea salt OR
1 tsp regular sea salt

2 eggs, beaten

100 g butter

150 ml sunflower oil

8 chicken thighs

Mix the flour with all the dry ingredients. Put the eggs in a shallow bowl and pour the seasoned flour onto a plate. Heat the butter and sunflower oil in a large frying pan until good and hot but not smoking. The chicken should hiss and sizzle but not roar as though you've dunked chips into a vat of oil.

Get a wire rack and place it over a baking tray for your chicken to sit on. Now, dip the chicken as follows: 1) flour, 2) egg, 3) flour, 4) egg, 5) flour. Sit them on the rack until they are all done and then fry in one or two batches for a good 10 minutes, turning them over gently so that they are a gorgeous golden brown colour. When they're all done, drain briefly on kitchen paper, sprinkle with a bit more sea salt and then bake in the oven for another 10 to 15 minutes while you tidy up.

Remove the shine from your face and serve it up on a big platter with paper plates and a bunch of napkins.

Garlic cream

3 heads garlic, peeled

Salt and pepper

2 tbsp olive oil

250 ml crème fraîche

1 tsp Tabasco sauce

1 lemon (optional)

Simmer the garlic cloves in boiling salted water for 10 minutes until tender. Drain, then mash or blend in a food processor with the olive oil and some salt. When it has cooled, whisk in the crème fraîche and Tabasco sauce. Season with salt and pepper and a squeeze of lemon juice if necessary.

Constance Spry's coronation chicken

Serves 4

1 medium chicken

Salt and pepper

1 onion, peeled and very finely chopped

2 tbsp olive oil

1 tbsp mild curry powder

Good squeeze tomato purée

150 ml red wine

120 ml water

1 bay leaf

1 tsp caster sugar

4 tbsp mayonnaise

2 tbsp mango chutney

Cooking something like coronation chicken is a great reminder of why certain dishes are 'classics'. A classic always tastes great whether you're a teenager or a pensioner – flavours like these simply never go out of style. The combination of curry powder slowly sweating with onions and red wine, before being added to mayonnaise, mango chutney and a delicious pile of poached, tender chicken, is really scrumptious.

As mentioned above, put the chicken in a large pot, cover with cold water, add some salt and pepper and bring it to the boil. Simmer very gently for 20 minutes (slosh out any scum) and then turn off the heat and leave the chicken to cook in the hot water for an hour. If your chicken is a giant, then simmer for another 5 minutes before turning off the heat.

When an hour has passed, carefully remove the bird (hot water will burn you while running down your hand if you're not careful). Strip away and discard the skin. Then tear the flesh off every nook and cranny, and set aside. Discard the carcass, but do boil down the chicken broth as this will make a fine light chicken stock for something else.

Meanwhile, make the coronation essence. Sweat the onions in the olive oil until soft. Add the curry powder and mix well. Turn up the heat and let it sizzle a bit (sizzle does not mean burn). After a minute or so, add the tomato purée and mix well. Then add the wine, water, bay leaf, some seasoning and the sugar. Mix well. Allow it to reduce down until it is thick and becomes a lovely rich dark colour. Allow it to cool down and then mix with the mayo and mango chutney.

Lightly dress the chicken and serve with crisp green leaves.

TIP: The leftover cooking stock is easy to reduce down, skim and use for soup. See page 101 for stracciatella.

Chinese spiced pork fillet

Serves 2–3

1 pork fillet (about 700 g)

100 ml soy sauce

50 ml dry sherry OR rice wine

2 tsp Chinese 5-spice powder

2 tsp brown sugar

Big piece ginger, peeled and very finely diced

4 cloves garlic, peeled and thinly sliced

Bunch spring onions, thinly sliced

Splash sunflower oil

The cooking method for this pork dish may seem a bit strange, but the end result is really soft, tender and slightly caramelised pork slices. It is very tasty, mainly because of all the soy sauce, ginger and garlic. It would go well with something very plain such as rice and steamed broccoli.

Trim any fat from the pork. It will be well trimmed anyway, but you'll always find a few shimmery bits of fat that would make it tough. So trim, discard and then very thinly slice the pork and put it in a bowl. Pour the soy sauce, sherry/rice wine, 5-spice powder, brown sugar, ginger, garlic and spring onions on top. Mix it about and leave to sit for a few minutes while you get some rice cooking or some broccoli blanching.

When you are ready to cook, heat up a large frying pan and throw the pork in. Let it 'stew/sauté' gently; there will be too much liquid for it to fry, so the idea is that it gently poaches in the soy sauce marinade. When you've tossed it around and it's cooked gently for about 5 minutes in total, drain the pork over a bowl, reserving the marinade. Then reheat the same frying pan, add in the sunflower oil and get it as hot as you can. Fry the drained pork quickly, toss around and, when you've got some good colour on the slices, chuck in the leftover cooking liquid, let it bubble away for a minute or two and then serve over rice.

TIP: You need to use Chinese 5-spice powder for this recipe but feel free to drastically increase the ginger/garlic and spring onion ratio.

Baked beans with chorizo, egg and feta

Serves 4

Olive oil

1 chorizo sausage, diced

2 onions, peeled and finely chopped

4 garlic cloves, peeled and finely chopped

Few sprigs thyme OR rosemary, finely chopped

80 ml red wine vinegar

4 tbsp tomato purée

2 x 450 g tins cannellini beans, drained and rinsed

4 large eggs

Approx. 200 g feta cheese

Salt and pepper

Cypriot/Greek food is mighty tasty, and full of some of my favourite ingredients, especially olives, chickpeas, feta cheese, grilled meats and halloumi. This convenient supper dish takes its inspiration from Greek cuisine, and derives from a recipe from Ozzie chef Karen Martini. It would also be perfect for brunch.

Combined with the plainer flavour of the eggs and beans, the super-tasty ingredients like feta and chorizo (okay, so chorizo is Spanish) work really well. All in all, a lip-smacking plate of savoury tastiness.

Preheat the oven to 180°C.

Heat a splash of olive oil in a large frying pan or saucepan and sauté the chorizo in a little olive oil until starting to caramelise. It does release lots of fat, which you can drain off if you're being good, or leave in there for extra unctuousness. Add the onions and continue to sauté until they too are just starting to colour. Add the garlic, herbs, red wine vinegar, tomato purée and 3 tablespoons of water. Mix well, season and cook for another few minutes. When everything feels well blended, take the pan off the heat and mix in the cannellini beans.

Transfer the mixtures to a gratin dish of some sort. Make four 'wells' or 'holes' in the beans and crack an egg into each well. Drizzle with more olive oil, crumble the feta cheese on top, season with lots of black pepper and bake for 15 minutes or so until the eggs are just cooked.

Serve with bread, and a salad, if you insist on some greens.

Lamb, beer and black bean chilli

Serves 4–6

Olive oil

750 g shoulder of lamb, cubed into big bite-sized chunks

Salt and pepper

1 large onion, peeled and chopped

4 cloves garlic, peeled and sliced

2 green chillies, finely sliced

2 tsp ground cumin

2 x 400 g tins tomatoes

300 ml bottle lager

1 tbsp tomato purée

1 tbsp soft brown sugar

3 tsp dried oregano

2 x 400 g tins black beans

Making dinner for someone really does mean a lot, and it's something that never fails to impress, no matter how simple or modest. Which is where this lamb chilli, taken from Diana Henry's *Food From Plenty*, comes in. This is a fabulous dish that also reheats splendidly. And don't fret: the tinned black beans work really well here, so no need for soaking the night before.

Heat a good glug of olive oil in a heavy-based saucepan and fry the lamb over a high heat so it browns all over. Season really well and keep the heat up high. When you have good colour, remove from the heat, spoon the lamb onto a plate and don't wash out the pan. Fry the onions in the same pan until soft, and season well. Add the garlic, chillies and cumin. Then add the lamb back to the pan and mix well so that everything gets really well coated in all the tasty stuff.

When it starts to smell good, add in the tomatoes, lager, tomato purée, sugar and oregano. Bring to a simmer, put a lid on and cook on a very gentle heat for 90 minutes. At that stage, add the beans and cook for another 30 minutes. I do the first part with a lid on and give it a gentle stir every now and then and leave the lid off for the second tranche of cooking, so that it can reduce down.

Let it cool down a bit to relax, and then taste. Like all stews, this tastes better if you can leave it to settle down for an hour or so (or overnight) and reheat. Overnight snoozing and next-day reheating works well when you want flavours to develop. Serve with rice and chopped coriander, or even on its own as the black beans stretch it out.

TIP: I often put chillies in the freezer as it seems to make them fairly mild and then I don't bother to deseed them and they're never too hot. They're also very easy to slice when frozen.

Meatloaf with crushed tomato sauce

Being a bona fide food nerd, I usually relish the opportunity to do a bit of research about food. But on this occasion, I have to say I couldn't believe what little interest I had in my chosen subject and I could barely bring myself to read about what must be the ugliest dish in the world as far as your eyes and ears are concerned: meatloaf. Meatloaf sure is no beauty contestant, but its humble (read ugly) appearance masks a really fantastic slice of flavour.

In my search for the best meatloaf recipe I could find, I settled on two contenders: Skye Gyngell's veal and pork one from *How I Cook*, and Pat Whelan's simpler beef and pork one in *An Irish Butcher Shop*. I ended up combining the best of both recipes but mine also has a tweaked version of Skye's tomato sauce, which is a great condiment for roast chicken, too.

Meatloaf

Serves 6–8

Olive oil

500 g minced beef

500 g minced pork

100 g breadcrumbs

3 cloves garlic, peeled and chopped

150 g Parmesan cheese, grated

1 tbsp sundried tomato paste

Good pinch chilli flakes

1–2 tbsp chopped herbs such as sage and thyme

Salt and pepper

. . . .

Approx. 500 g cherry OR vine tomatoes

80 ml olive oil

3 cloves garlic, peeled and crushed

Big bunch parsley, finely chopped

Salt and pepper

2 tbsp Dijon mustard

200 g black olives, roughly chopped

Few splashes Tabasco sauce

1 tsp caster sugar

Preheat the oven to 190°C. Oil the loaf tin. I use a 23 x 13 cm non-stick loaf tin.

Mix all the ingredients (excluding the salt and pepper) together. To take the guesswork out of it, you should fry a little blob of the mixture, so you can taste it and adjust the seasoning. The Parmesan cheese and sundried tomato paste are quite salty, but there's one kilo of minced meats in there, too, so it does need to be seasoned. But if you're confident enough, just chuck in some salt and pepper, pour or rather push the meat into the loaf tin and then bake for about an hour.

I cover it with tinfoil at the beginning, cook it for about 40 minutes and then remove the foil for the last 20 minutes so that it can brown on top. It stays beautifully moist even though it cooks for nearly an hour.

Cool slightly, turn out onto a platter, slice and serve with the sauce. I also let it cool down fully and heat up some leftover slices with some extra grated Parmesan cheese the next day and it is just as good, if not better.

Crushed tomato sauce

Slice the tomatoes in half and scatter on a roasting tin. Drizzle with a splash of olive oil. When the meatloaf is about 20 minutes away from the end of its cooking time, bake the tomatoes until slightly charring. Transfer to a bowl. Add in the rest of the ingredients and mix well but try not to break up the tomatoes too much. Taste, season and serve with the meatloaf.

Cuban black beans and rice with bacon

Serves 6–8

500 g black beans (also known as black turtle beans)

Salt

1.5 litre chicken stock (can be of the cubed variety)

2 bay leaves

12 smoked bacon rashers, diced

4 tbsp olive oil

4 tsp cumin seeds

½ head garlic, peeled and finely chopped

1 large onion, peeled and chopped

2 green peppers, deseeded and diced

500 g long-grain white rice

4 tbsp red wine vinegar

1 tbsp oregano leaves OR 2 tsp dried oregano

Good squeeze tomato ketchup

Bunch spring onions

Lime wedges

I'm a big fan of using tinned beans at home, so a little forward planning is required when a recipe calls for pulses and legumes that require overnight soaking and hours of boiling, especially when the tinned option doesn't serve the dish at all well.

This recipe reminds me of my childhood in the West Indies, where I was born and where this dish was called 'peas and rice'. I'm not sure why I hadn't tried to make it until recently, but when I came across a recipe in an American food magazine, I had a real urge to savour those flavours again. As soon as I tasted it, I was immediately transported back to somewhere light, breezy and extremely sunny. This is really delicious, hearty food, and although you could leave out the bacon if you're vegetarian, you'll find that throughout that neck of the woods, pork is a firm favourite with the locals (as it is in Ireland) and it lends great body to the dish.

Soak the black beans in generously salted water for 8 to 10 hours. Drain and rinse well. Cook the beans in the stock along with the bay leaves for 30 to 40 minutes. Drain the beans over a bowl as you need to reserve this cooking liquor.

Preheat the oven to 180°C.

In a large, heavy-based saucepan, fry the bacon in about half the olive oil. Once it starts to brown and caramelise, add the cumin and garlic and possibly the rest of the olive oil if you feel it needs a little more fat in the pan. Then add the onions and green peppers. Keep the heat up high and allow this mixture to sweat and soften. The flavour of the bacon fat should coat the mirepoix of vegetables and the garlic needs to cook out as well. You don't really want these vegetables to brown, just to soften and bring out some sweetness.

Rinse the rice really well under a tap until the water runs clear to help remove excess starch. Drain and chuck the rice into the saucepan and add the reserved cooking liquor (which will be an inky black). Add the black beans. The stock should be enough to turn it into a sloppy stew, rather than a watery bath. Add the vinegar, oregano and ketchup. Cover with a lid and bake for 30 to 40 minutes. Check the rice about halfway and if you think you need to add more liquid, do so. Basically it should end up like a pilaf, but if it's too wet, then just remove the lid for a while.

The main thing is that it's super tasty and that the rice is cooked through. If you mix it too much it will get a bit sticky, but season well and if it's too bland, then add more vinegar, salt, pepper and oregano.

Serve with chopped spring onions, a squeeze of lime juice and a beer, while listening to some Bob Marley.

Sesame trout with pea pesto

We're always being told how good oily fish is for us, so in the interest of eating more of it, here is a great recipe for trout, tweaked from one by Sarah Raven. The pea pesto is a great accompaniment that is very easy to make, and it was also lovely on sourdough toast with a little shaved Parmesan cheese and extra olive oil.

Sesame trout

Serves 4

40 g sesame seeds, lightly toasted

Salt and pepper

2 tbsp olive oil

2 trout OR salmon fillets, skinned (approx. 200 g each)

1 knob butter

1 tbsp toasted sesame oil

Spread the sesame seeds on a large plate and season with lots of salt and pepper. Meanwhile heat the olive oil in a large non-stick frying pan. Dip the fish onto the seeds to coat it on one side. Fry it in the olive oil, seeded side down. Season with more salt and pepper and then add in the knob of butter to help give colour and flavour. You'll be able to turn it over to get some searing on the other side. Add the sesame oil when you're just about finished cooking. These take only a few minutes on each side, but if you like them really well cooked, I'd transfer them to a hot oven (say 180°C) for another 5 minutes or so as the seeds can start to burn and the trout will complete its cooking better in the oven.

Pea pesto

300 g frozen peas

Large handful basil

Juice of 1 lemon

1 tbsp ginger, peeled and grated

3 cloves garlic, peeled

Salt and pepper

2–3 tbsp olive oil

2–3 tbsp water

Squeeze honey

Thaw the peas or blanch quickly and refresh in cold water. When cold, process them with the rest of the ingredients. Season well and serve. This pesto will keep for a few hours in the fridge but doesn't do too well left there for long.

Chicken casserole with mustard and smoked paprika

Serves 4

50 g butter

4 chicken legs with thigh attached

Salt and pepper

50 ml white wine vinegar

2 tbsp Dijon mustard

1 tbsp wholegrain mustard

300 ml chicken stock

50 ml cream

2 tsp dried oregano

½ tsp smoked sweet paprika

Few sprigs rosemary

4 cloves garlic, peeled and crushed

2 bay leaves

When temperatures drop, I find myself reaching for everything that was abandoned during the summer. So in chillier weather, the recipe for rabbit legs braised with mustard in Anthony Demetre's *Today's Special* will send you racing to the butcher. But, perhaps because most butchers don't regularly stock legs from the cast of *Watership Down*, I've tweaked it to use chicken legs instead, which work just as well and eat beautifully. Use chicken legs with leg and thigh still attached or else about six drumsticks.

This is an incredibly tasty dish, and it can be cooked on top of the stove, provided you have a good heavy saucepan with a lid, or, if it's handier, in the oven. The other thing is to wipe out all the fat after you've browned the chicken legs. We just don't need to unnecessarily consume animal fats, especially if it's not doing anything incredible to the dish.

Melt the butter in a heavy-based saucepan. Season the chicken legs well and fry them over a high heat until a golden brown and even colour on all sides. This will take a good 5 to 10 minutes. Transfer them to a plate and discard all the fat in the saucepan. Wipe the saucepan clean and then add the vinegar and boil until bubbling for about a minute. Then add all the remaining ingredients, whisk so that it is well mixed. Bring to the boil. Taste and adjust the seasoning if necessary and then gently place the chicken legs back into the saucepan. Put the lid on and either cook on top of the stove over a low heat for about 25 minutes or bake in the oven at 160°C for about 40 minutes. It should be bubbling away gently, but do keep an eye on it.

Take the casserole off the heat or out of the oven, allow to cool for a bit, and serve with some bread to dunk into the sauce or some wild rice.

Pork schnitzel

Serves 4

Salt and pepper

2 eggs, beaten

1 clove garlic, peeled and crushed

½ tsp smoked sweet paprika

1 tsp dried oregano OR thyme

1 trimmed pork tenderloin, cut into 2 cm thick slices

100 g breadcrumbs

Good few knobs butter

2–3 tbsp sunflower OR rapeseed oil

Lemon wedges to serve

Normally when making schnitzel, the meat is dipped in flour, then egg, then breadcrumbs. I skip the flour stage and, to be honest, you don't really notice, but feel free to include it if you're fussy about even coatings. I'm very resistant to frying anything (even shallow frying) and really have to be keen on making something to justify flouring and dipping in egg and breadcrumbs. So, by eliminating one step, I feel much less like some indentured slave on a flour, egg and crumb conveyor belt.

The schnitzel are great with some buttered noodles or just a squeeze of lemon juice or even some celeriac remoulade (see page 43) or green salad.

Preheat the oven to 180°C.

Season the eggs and add the garlic, paprika and dried herbs. Whisk well. Put the slices of pork between two sheets of clingfilm (or in a heavy-duty zip-lock lunch bag) and bash with a rolling pin until nearly double in size. When they are all done, drop the pork into the seasoned egg mixture. Wash the boards and utensils carefully and get a plate or tray of breadcrumbs set up. You can do this step up to 12 hours in advance.

When you're ready for final cooking, heat about one tablespoon of oil in a large frying pan and add a knob of butter. Then remove a couple of pieces of pork from the egg mixture and dip the pork into the breadcrumbs. Press the pork into the breadcrumbs, so that they stick well, and then fry a few at a time. When they are golden brown and crisp on one side, turn them over. When evenly coloured, you can place them on a baking tray ready to finish cooking in the oven.

Halfway through frying, you may have to wipe out the oil and start again with fresh oil and butter, as the loose breadcrumbs can start to burn quite easily. When all the pork has been fried, season them lightly and bake in the oven for about 10 minutes.

Serve while still hot with lemon wedges. The schnitzel are also delicious eaten cold, and when reheated in the oven for about 20 minutes the next day, they are still delicious, if a bit dried out.

Roast lamb with lemon, oregano and garlic

Serves 6

2kg leg of lamb, boned

Handful basil leaves

Handful oregano leaves OR 1 tsp dried oregano

10 cloves garlic, peeled

150 ml olive oil

1 (30 g) tin of anchovies, drained

Rind and juice of 2 lemons

60 g ground almonds

Salt and pepper

This recipe for roast lamb is so yummy that it has even been known to convert a few lambatarians (we've got a teenage one at home). Lambatarians seem to have no problem tucking into bacon (despite reminders about *Babe* and *Charlotte's Web*) or any kind of steak or hamburger. But a drive through the countryside in spring, when one can see baby lambs frolicking around, pogoing the land, can have a long-lasting effect. However, even die-hard lovers of lambs will happily scoff through this dish.

If you want to do it old school, like I do, then get a boned leg of lamb and score the fat on the outside with a sharp knife, but don't go through the flesh. Whizz the herbs, garlic and olive oil (which you should slowly pour in) in a blender until smooth-ish. I also like to add in a few anchovies or even a small tin of drained anchovies. They give the lamb a really great flavour, with none of the 'fishiness' you might expect. Stir in the lemon rind and juice, ground almonds and loads of black pepper. Smear this all over the lamb and leave overnight, if possible, in a non-metallic bowl or even a plastic bag.

Bring the lamb to room temperature before seasoning with plenty of salt and roasting on a high heat (220°C) for about 20 minutes. Then reduce the heat to 180°C and cook for a further 20 minutes. Leave to rest somewhere warm for another 20 minutes and then slice thinly and serve with your favourite carbohydrate or, for ultimate laziness, with some hummus slathered between some slices of crusty bread with loads of peppery salad leaves.

Garvan's tomato and chorizo pasta

Serves 4

100 ml olive oil

6 cloves garlic

Salt and pepper

1 decent chorizo sausage

250 g of the juiciest, sweetest, ripest baby tomatoes

1 tsp demerara sugar

500 g penne pasta

Most couples I know seem to have a relatively decent household chore-sharing thing going on. And more often than one would think, I find it's the blokes who do more cooking, with well-fed partners quite happy to wash up in return. In my home, I do most of the cooking, which works for us, but there are times when I'm extremely grateful to have a plate of food plonked in front of me, especially when I'm tired, grumpy and starving, with looming deadlines and children on the loose.

So, despite my husband's pathetic attempts to wriggle out of cooking, I find that like most people who say they don't particularly enjoy cooking, he's got a couple of dishes that he does especially well. This chorizo and pasta dish is fantastically tasty and one of my favourites, mainly because a bit of time and care goes into chopping the chorizo and tomatoes into very small chunks and preserving every little bit of tomato juice that spills onto the chopping board. It's a dish that's bullish, rustic and very delicious.

Heat the olive oil, very gently, while you hunker down and peel and crush the garlic and chop the chorizo into very small pieces or cubes – the smaller the better. Do the same with the baby or cherry tomatoes. Next, add the garlic to the oil and gently poach in the oil. Season this oil and garlic mixture very well. Cook very gently, so no colouring the garlic. Add the chorizo and then the chopped tomatoes, making sure that all the juice and bits go into the pan, and then add the sugar. Cook slowly for about 30 minutes on the gentlest of heats.

When you're ready, cook the penne in plenty of boiling water, drain, splash with some olive oil and toss with the pasta sauce. Serving with lots of Parmesan cheese and a beefy red wine makes this a very moreish supper.

sweet treats

One of my favourite old cookbooks is Maura Laverty's *Kind Cooking*, which dates back to the 1950s and is full not only of old-fashioned recipes, but also of wise words about the joys of home cooking. Her introduction states that 'every little girl born into this world loves to help in the kitchen'. Although we can shout that boys and dads are included nowadays, it's important not to get distracted from the pearls of wisdom she's keen to share.

The point she makes is that unless children are encouraged to cook, they will struggle to find it interesting, and it's up to us as parents to help nurture this interest. As she reminds us, it's so important for mums (and dads, aunts, uncles, brothers and sisters!) 'to look backwards and forwards – back to her own childhood and the thrill that came from being allowed to help, forward to the day when her daughter will be grown up and when cooking will be as much a duty as a pleasure'.

With those words ringing in my ear, I try to do the same. After all, it's what my mum did for me.

Apricot and pistachio cake with poached apricots

Anyone who reads my column in *The Irish Times* will know that I am a most reluctant baker, but some recipes just make it so easy that it leaves me with no excuse worth entertaining. This cake, taken from Tom Kime's *Exploring Taste and Flavour*, is one of those, mainly because the poached apricots taste so good. They are actually tasty enough to serve just with some Greek yoghurt. I'll do anything to avoid baking a cake!

Serves 8

150 g pistachios, without skins

150 g plain flour

¾ tsp bicarbonate of soda

¼ tsp baking powder

Good pinch salt

Zest of one lemon

6 eggs, separated

225 g caster sugar

150 ml plain yoghurt

150 ml olive oil

200 g dried apricots

1 cinnamon stick

1 tbsp honey

1 tbsp brown sugar

Seeds from 1 vanilla pod

Juice and zest of 1 orange

600 ml water

½ tsp all-spice

1 tsp ground black pepper

Apricot and pistachio cake

Preheat the oven to 180°C. Grease a 25 cm spring-form cake tin.

Grind up the pistachio nuts. Sieve the dry ingredients and add the lemon zest. Beat the egg yolks with half the sugar until pale and creamy. Add the yoghurt, olive oil and then fold in the flour and pistachio nuts. Whisk the egg whites until soft peaks form. Gradually add the remaining sugar and beat until stiff. Fold the egg whites into the cake mix and then pour into the cake tin. Bake for 50 to 55 minutes until a knife comes out clean.

Poached apricots

Put all the ingredients into a saucepan, heat gently and simmer for 10 minutes. Allow to cool slightly, remove the apricots and reduce the sugar syrup by one-third. Add the apricots back to the syrup and then allow to cool fully. Serve with the warm pistachio cake.

Cherry and cinnamon cake

Serves 8

500 g cherries
140 g self-raising flour
½ tsp ground cinnamon
50 g caster sugar
1 egg
100 ml milk
85g butter, melted

Topping:
25 g cream flour
50 g soft brown sugar
½ tsp cinnamon
25 g butter, diced

I don't think too hard about what variety of cherries I should be buying as it's usually only the dark, sweet juicy ones that hit our shops in mid-summer. Occasionally you see the speckled yellowish ones, but I tend to focus on the lusciously sinister and seductive looking cherries that resemble something Snow White would pig out on. What happens next for me is a cherry binge, but thankfully the stones in cherries keep the pace of my consumption within speed limits.

Cherries contain lots of antioxidants and vitamin C, and the evidence seems to be mounting that they also help reduce inflammation and help fight certain cancers, heart disease and diabetes. They contain lots of melatonin, which is good for everything from jet lag to memory loss. So the bottom line is this: when you see them, buy them, wash them well and happily gorge on them. When you think they're on the verge of turning on you, then try this recipe.

Preheat the oven to 180°C. Butter and line the base of a 25 cm spring-form cake tin.

Stone the cherries, which should leave you with 450 g. In a bowl, mix the flour with the cinnamon and sugar. Make a well in the centre and mix in the egg, milk and melted butter. I do this with a whisk for a minute. Once it is a thick smooth batter, pour it into the prepared tin. Top with the cherries and lightly press down.

Prepare the topping in another clean bowl: mix the flour with the sugar and cinnamon. Add in the diced butter and, using your fingertips, lightly mix the butter and dry ingredients together so that they form a crumb. Top the cake with the crumb mixture and bake for 35 to 40 minutes.

Tastes great the next day.

Strawberry tart

Serves 8

250 g plain flour
125 g butter
30 g caster sugar
2 egg yolks
Zest of 1 lemon
1 tsp vanilla extract

Crème pâtissière:
5 egg yolks
Seeds from 1 vanilla pod
120 g caster sugar
50 g plain flour
425 ml milk
30 g butter
250 ml crème fraîche
50 g icing sugar

500 g hulled strawberries
2 tbsp redcurrant jelly

Is there anything better and more summery than Irish strawberries in summer? This is one of those strawberry desserts that it would be a shame not to make when the season is in full swing. And don't worry if your pastry skills are not that fantastic. You can use a readymade pastry case or even some individual ones and just fill it up with crème pâtissière and a tonne of berries. The more, the merrier. Enjoy!

To make the pastry, pulse the flour, butter and sugar in a food processor until it forms breadcrumbs. Then add in the egg yolks, lemon zest and vanilla extract. Process until it forms a ball of dough. If you have to add a splash of water to get this to happen, go ahead. Wrap in clingfilm and chill for 30 minutes (or overnight if you fancy).

Preheat the oven to 180°C. Roll out the pastry between two big sheets of clingfilm. Then line a 25 cm tart tin, prick the base with a fork and chill for another 20 minutes. Line with scrunched-up baking parchment and fill with dried beans or rice. Blind bake for 20 minutes.

Remove from the oven, carefully lift out the beans and paper and then put the pastry back in the oven for another 10 to 15 minutes or until nice and golden brown and dry. Allow to cool in the tin and set aside until you are ready to fill it. I find it's easier to fill and decorate when it's still in the tin (providing it's one of those tart tins with a removable base). It just keeps everything more stable. You can remove it from the tin and plonk it on a plate or cake stand when it's closer to the time of serving up.

To make the crème pâtissière: whisk the egg yolks and seeds from the vanilla pod along with the sugar until pale and thick. Whisk in the flour. Meanwhile, boil the milk and then slowly pour onto the egg mixture, whisking all the time. When all the milk has been incorporated, transfer to a non-stick saucepan and keep stirring or whisking and slowly bring to the boil. Simmer gently, while stirring for a couple of minutes, then remove from the heat and put into a bowl to cool.

'Wipe' or rub the surface of the crème pâtissière with the butter so that a film of butter coats the surface, which will help prevent a skin from forming. When at room temperature, fold in the crème fraîche and icing sugar to taste.

To assemble: fill the pastry shell with the crème pâtissière and decorate with the hulled strawberries. For the final touch, warm up the redcurrant jelly with one tablespoon of boiling water and, when loose enough, brush carefully to glaze the berries. Serve in big wedges.

Banana puddings with toffee sauce

Serves 6

150 g soft butter

150 g demerara sugar

3 medium eggs, beaten

3 large over-ripe bananas, mushed

150 g plain white flour

1 tsp baking powder

Toffee sauce:

50 g butter

50 g demerara sugar

3 tbsp golden syrup

125 ml cream

These banana puddings are like little mounds of banana bread soaked with toffee: in other words, a good combo. For lovers of a more traditional sticky toffee pudding, this cake is my own wily creation. And the sauce would make old socks taste good.

Preheat the oven to 180°C.

First, make the toffee sauce. Melt the butter and sugar and, when the sugar dissolves, whisk in the golden syrup and cream. Simmer for a minute, whisking every now and then and then set aside until you've made the puddings.

Grease six 200 ml dariole moulds and then line with small sheets of greaseproof paper that you've crumpled up and dampened slightly, which makes it easier. If you don't line them with greaseproof paper, they may stick a bit, but it's not the end of the world as you can ease them out with a sharp knife.

Beat the butter and sugar with an electric beater until light and fluffy. Add the eggs and banana and beat until well mixed. Don't worry if it curdles. Add a spoonful of flour to it and continue to beat. Fold in the rest of the flour and the baking powder, which you can sieve into the bowl.

Starting with a spoon of sauce, layer up the moulds with alternate spoonfuls of pudding mix and sauce. Put the moulds on a baking tray and bake for 20 to 25 minutes. Serve warm with cream, any leftover sauce and some chopped nuts.

TIP: This pudding tastes much better after a day or two and can be reheated in the tin or even in the microwave for a few seconds.

Cinnamon and brown sugar crème brûlée ice cream

Serves 4–6

200 ml milk

375 ml cream

1 tsp vanilla extract

Good pinch cinnamon

5 egg yolks

120 g caster sugar

2–3 tbsp demerara sugar

Adapted from a Rick Stein recipe, this ice cream is so rich and delicious that you can eat only a small amount. I love crème brulée, but unless you have a blow-torch at home, they just don't work under the grill. However, this recipe works without a blow-torch as the eventual aim is to make ice cream rather than crème brûlée, so once you freeze the custard down a bit, it's safe to brûlée under your grill and then re-freeze before smashing it up a bit, so that the shards of caramel are mixed through.

In a non-stick saucepan, heat the milk, cream, vanilla and cinnamon until just coming to the boil. Take off the heat.

Meanwhile, whisk the egg yolks and caster sugar with an electric beater until thick, pale and creamy, which will take about 4 minutes. Stir in the cream and milk with a wooden spoon or whisk by hand. Then wash out the non-stick saucepan. Pour the custard mixture back into the clean non-stick saucepan and heat very gently until the mixture thickens slightly, and coats the back of a wooden spoon. This takes a little time, especially if you start out on a low heat. Nothing will happen for about 2 minutes and then, suddenly, you will feel the texture change and get slightly 'heavy'. Take it off the heat and keep stirring gently. If it does start to hint at scrambling, you can always sieve it. But there are plenty of textures in this dish, so even if you get a few blobs of what looks suspiciously like scrambled eggs, don't panic. Just be sure to keep taking it off the heat and stirring. Take your time with this bit.

Pour into a shallow gratin dish and, when cooled down to room temperature, put it in the fridge overnight.

An hour before you want to brulée it, put the gratin dish in the freezer. Then sprinkle with the demerara sugar and grill until caramelised and deep golden brown. Freeze for at least a few hours and then smash up with a fork and re-freeze for another couple of hours.

Pear, apple and ginger muffins

Makes 12–16

Sunflower oil for greasing

3 dessert apples (approx. 400 g), peeled, cored and diced (approx. 240 g)

1 tsp ground ginger

1 tsp ground cinnamon

¼ tsp nutmeg

2 tsp baking powder

145 g wholegrain spelt flour

150 g rolled outs

4 egg whites, lightly beaten until frothy

125 ml plain yoghurt

240 g agave syrup OR honey

110 g raisins

1 pear, peeled and diced

Always on the search for good breakfast and brunch items, I came up with this muffin recipe based on one in Sophie Dahl's very useful cookbook *Miss Dahl's Voluptuous Delights*, tweaking it a good bit to make it even more holier-than-thou good for you. Initially I felt like a bit of a neurotic Hollywood-type for endorsing them, as they are made with egg whites and yoghurt (rather than butter, sunflower oil and whole eggs), but when you're craving a bit of comfort food and don't want to go overboard on the fat factor, they are perfect.

I used wholegrain spelt flour simply because it's all they had in the shops when I went in search of 'spelt flour'. You could also use plain old white spelt flour or cream flour.

Preheat the oven to 190°C. Grease a non-stick 12-muffin tray with a little sunflower oil. You could get 16 muffins out of this recipe, or over-stuff the tin for 12.

Cook the diced apple with 150 ml water on a gentle heat for about 10 minutes until you have dry apple mush. Meanwhile, mix the spices with the baking powder, flour and oats. Make a well in the centre. In another bowl, lightly whisk the egg whites together with the yoghurt, agave syrup/honey and apple mush. Pour these wet ingredients into the well of dried ingredients. Mix gently and fold in the raisins and diced pear. Fill up the muffin tray and bake for 25 minutes or so until golden brown.

Key lime pie

Serves 8–10

300 g digestives

100 g butter, melted

8 egg yolks

2 x 397 g tins sweetened condensed milk

Juice and zest of 10 limes

Small bunch mint (optional), finely chopped

Approx. 450 ml cream

A very nice lady emailed a while back and insisted I try out the key lime pie recipe from *The Hummingbird Bakery Cookbook*. It's a very sweet book, full of cutesy cookies, pies and, naturally, the ubiquitous cupcake.

Now, according to my little bit of online research, it seems that the original recipe for key lime pie required small key limes, found in the Florida Keys, which have a thin yellow rind but are incredibly tart and aromatic, with a pale yellow juice. Luckily for those of us not fortunate enough to live in balmy Florida, regular old limes work just as well.

Anyway, the famed Hummingbird recipe was tried and the volume on the lime-juice quotient was turned up a notch or two. I also add some mint for pure devilment, which is quite nice, though do feel free to leave it out.

Preheat the oven to 170°C.

Whizz the digestives and the melted butter, on pulse mode, in a food processor until it forms a fine crumb. Press into a 29 cm tart tin, with a removable base, and bake for 20 minutes and then cool.

Reduce the oven to 150°C. Beat the egg yolks with the condensed milk, lime juice and zest. If you're going to add mint, then do so now. Pour the mixture into the tart tin, which should be sitting on a baking tray so you can transport it easily. Bake for 20 to 30 minutes until just set and jelly-like. Cool to room temperature and then refrigerate until cold and set.

When ready to serve, whip the cream until thick and smother on top. Decorate with some lime zest if you're feeling fancy.

Rhubarb and honey cream tart

Serves 8

225 g flour
40 g icing sugar
150 g butter
1 large egg, beaten

Filling:
2–3 large sticks of
rhubarb (approx. 300 g)
2 tbsp caster sugar
4 egg yolks
300 ml cream
Pinch saffron
6 tbsp honey
1 tsp vanilla extract

When April comes and rhubarb is in season, I simply can't resist eating it as often as possible, in tarts, compotes, crumbles or any other form. This rhubarb tart is one I've altered slightly from a recipe by my pal Rachel Allen. It looks absolutely gorgeous and is really delicious, although the pastry is quite tricky to handle. The end result is very much worth any slight frustration you'll have when lining your tin, however.

First, make the pastry. Mix the flour, icing sugar, butter and egg together in a food processor. When it forms a ball, wrap in clingfilm and leave it to rest for at least an hour, but preferably overnight. Roll out the pastry and carefully line a 25 cm tart tin then chill again for another hour while you preheat the oven to 180°C. Scrunch up some greaseproof paper and place it on top of the pastry with some dried beans or rice. Blind bake for 15 minutes. Carefully remove the paper and beans (they will be very hot) and bake the pastry for another 5 minutes to dry out. Leave to cool down while you make the filling.

Trim the rhubarb and then chop into 1 cm chunks. You should be left with 250 g chopped, perfect chunks. Toss with the caster sugar. Whisk the egg yolks with the cream, saffron, honey and vanilla, then pour into the tart case (which should be sitting on a baking tray for ease of transporting). Carefully place rhubarb strategically around the circle, to form a pretty pattern. Place them so that one cut side faces up. Bake for 35 minutes at 180°C. There should still be a little wobble in the filling, which will solidify once it has cooled down.

Delicious with whipped cream or vanilla ice cream.

Rich dark chocolate mousse

Serves 6

300 g dark chocolate

150 g butter

6 eggs, separated

150 ml cream

80 g caster sugar

Chocolate mousse is always a winner. This dark chocolate version is a great one for kids to make because it's dead easy and is lovely served in glasses. However, it does need a good few hours to set so that it loses its gooiness and instead takes on a dense fudginess that is really gorgeous with a coffee – for the adults!

Break the chocolate into small pieces. Melt the chocolate and butter in a glass bowl over a pan of simmering water. When melted and slightly cooled, beat in the egg yolks with a wooden spoon. It will go quite thick and shiny so keep stirring and then gradually add in the cream, which you should heat up first, separately in a saucepan. (If you don't, the chocolate seizes up for a few minutes and it all looks a bit dodgy. But once you fold in the egg whites, all comes good.) Whisk the egg whites until they form soft peaks and then add in the sugar, spoonful by spoonful. Fold into the chocolate mixture. At this stage, it should be shiny and smooth.

Divide between six glasses, chill overnight and serve.

Nigella's everyday brownies

Makes 8–10

150 g butter

300 g light brown muscovado sugar

1 tsp instant coffee granules

75 g cocoa

150 g plain flour

1 tsp bicarbonate of soda

4 eggs, beaten

1 tsp vanilla extract

200 g good milk chocolate, cut into chunks

Brownies are one of those things few people can resist. There's something about that combo of crumbly, slightly chewy crust and the dense fudginess within that appeals to everyone, especially children.

And children love making them, too. My nipper loves these ones from Nigella Lawson's book *Kitchen*. Her everyday brownies are great, though we did tweak a few bits, namely the amount of chocolate, and we also added some instant coffee and reduced the oven temperatures. They're gooey and delicious and are great to cook over half-term hols, as the methodology is very manageable, no matter how novice the chef.

Preheat the oven to 180°C. Line a 21 cm square cake tin with parchment paper.

Gently heat the butter and sugar together until the butter melts and the sugar starts to dissolve. Add the coffee granules. Sieve together the cocoa, flour and bicarbonate of soda. Add in stages to the melted butter and mix well. It will be like soft cement. Add the eggs and vanilla and it will become thick and glossy. None of the above methodology requires any finesse. Just get on with it. At this stage though, your tin needs to be ready to go. You just add in the chocolate chunks, give them a cursory mix and then pour straight into the tin and bake for 25 minutes.

It will puff up significantly but will be gooey and wobbly and the skewer won't come out clean, which Nigella says is the whole point! Leave them to cool slightly and serve with a strong coffee (for the adults) or ice cream (for everyone).

Chocolate, hazelnut and muscovado tart

Serves 8

100 g hazelnuts
100 g dark muscovado sugar
120 g flour
50 g soft butter
300 g dark chocolate
500 ml cream
6 egg yolks
200 g caster sugar

This is a great dinner-party dessert. I've also made this using rice flour instead of the regular flour, which I believe is okay for certain coeliacs to eat.

Preheat the oven to 140°C. You'll need a 24 cm tart tin with a removable base.

Toast the hazelnuts in the oven for 5 to 10 minutes until they are lightly done. Let them cool down a bit and whizz them in the food processor along with the muscovado sugar, flour and butter. Whizz until it forms a breadcrumb-like texture.

Press the crumbs into the tart tin, as you would a biscuity cheesecake base. Spread evenly, which is sometimes easier to do with a wet spatula, and then freeze or chill while you get the chocolate filling sorted.

Melt the dark chocolate in a bowl over simmering water. While that is melting, bring the cream just up to the boil. Whisk the egg yolks and sugar until pale, thick and doubled in volume. Pour the hot cream onto the melted chocolate and whisk. This will look scarily seized up for a second or two but keep whisking. Then fold the melted chocolate into the whisked egg yolks. It should become very thick and glossy as it's mixed in and starts to cool down slightly.

Put the tart tin onto a flat baking sheet, which will be easier to transport. Pour the chocolate filling in and bake for about 45 minutes. There will be a slight wobble in the middle, but this is gorgeous after it's cooled right down and served cold with a big blob of cream to which you've softly whipped in some vanilla extract and icing sugar.

Flourless chocolate and coffee cake

Serves 6–8

350 g dark chocolate, broken up

250 g caster sugar

180 ml boiling water

225 g butter

6 eggs, separated

2 tsp instant coffee

2 tsp vanilla extract

This is based on a lovely Sophie Dahl recipe. I used a 23 cm spring-form cake tin, which I didn't bother lining with parchment paper, but that's probably because I was feeling brave as it was a brand-new cake tin. My other ones are all a bit bashed, so would probably leak, in which case lining with parchment would definitely be a good call.

Preheat the oven to 180°C.

In a food processor, mix the broken-up chocolate and the sugar until it resembles coarse crumbs. Pour in the boiling water and whisk. Then add the egg yolks, coffee and vanilla.

Using an electric beater, whisk the egg whites until they form soft peaks. Fold in the chocolate mixture. Then pour into the cake tin and bake for about 45 minutes.

It really needs to cool down fully and is delicious eaten cold, straight from the fridge. Fudgy and moreish.

Strawberry and black pepper ice cream with brown sugar meringues

This isn't an attempt to be a bit poncey. Black pepper and strawberries make a great combo, but please feel free to throw your eyes to heaven and leave the pepper out if you wish.

Serves 6–8

At least 600 g strawberries

Juice of 1 orange

Juice of 1 lemon

500 ml cream

200 g caster sugar

Black pepper

Strawberry and black pepper ice cream

Hull the strawberries, chuck them into a food processor and blitz on pulse for a minute. Add the rest of the ingredients and whizz until the cream thickens up a bit. Season with lots of black pepper and freeze in a plastic container.

Sunflower oil

6 egg whites

200 g demerara sugar

1 tsp vanilla extract

Brown sugar meringues

Preheat the oven to 110°C. Line two baking trays with baking parchment, which you should rub with some sunflower oil.

Whisk the egg whites and when they form soft peaks, add in the sugar in stages and continue to beat until all the sugar is added and the meringue is stiff. Add in the vanilla extract. Spoon big blobs of the meringue onto the paper and bake for about 2 hours. Let them cool down in the oven.

Keep in an airtight container until ready to serve with the ice cream.

Spiced peach crumble

Serves 6

6 peaches, stoned and
thinly sliced

Juice of 1 lemon

1 tsp vanilla extract

2 tbsp caster sugar

Knob butter

Approx. 250 g raspberries

100 g plain flour

125 g ground almonds

125 g light muscovado
sugar

½ tsp ground cinnamon

150 g cold butter, cut into
cubes

Queen Elizabeth allegedly tells guests who complain that it's chilly in Balmoral to go and put on a sweater. I'm a bit the same about desserts. If anyone looks a bit longingly for something sweet after they've been fed dinner, they're promptly told to go find some dark chocolate in the cupboard and to leave me alone.

In summer, though, when the stores are full of peaches and raspberries, I can't resist this lovely Annie Bell recipe. It is really magical with a big blob of vanilla ice cream. I know crumbles may seem a bit too wintry when the sun is shining, but perhaps because of the acidity of the raspberries and richness of the peaches, this feels perfectly lovely to eat even when it isn't lashing rain outside. Maybe it's just an Irish thing, for we sure do love our crumbles.

Preheat the oven to 160°C.

Toss the sliced peaches with the lemon juice, vanilla extract and caster sugar in a bowl until well coated. Butter a large gratin dish (approx. 34 cm in length) and then chuck in the peaches. Arrange the raspberries on top, scattered all over the peaches. Set aside.

Put the flour, almonds, muscovado sugar and cinnamon in a food processor and whizz until they are well mixed. Add in the butter cubes and pulse until the mixture resembles breadcrumbs. Alternatively you could do this by hand, mixing the butter with the tips of your fingers, rubbing it into the flour mixture, remembering to keep your hands high and work lightly with your fingers so that the pastry stays in the form of breadcrumbs.

Top the fruit with the crumble topping and bake for 50 minutes until golden brown. Cool slightly and serve.

This is also delicious cold the next morning as a very decadent breakfast with a big blob of yoghurt.

Sticky toffee bread and butter pudding

Serves 6

200 g stoned dates

½ tsp bicarbonate of soda

12 slices white bread

75 g butter, very soft

3 eggs

3 egg yolks

75 g caster sugar

1 vanilla pod OR 1 tsp vanilla essence

500 ml cream

Sprinkle demerara sugar

Sticky toffee sauce:

100 g butter

100 g golden syrup

100 g soft dark brown sugar

100 ml crème fraîche

This sticky toffee pudding is based on the recipe from the cookbook for the British TV series *Great British Menu*. I would recommend doing this in a big gratin dish (about 28 x 16 cm, base measurements) rather than faffing around with individual portions.

Heat the dates with about 300 ml water and the bicarbonate of soda. The water should just cover the dates. Simmer for about 5 to 10 minutes until the mixture is quite dry and the texture is mushy but still 'spreadable'. Cut the crusts off the bread, butter it generously on both sides and put 6 slices on the base of the gratin dish. Hopefully they will snugly fit in one neat layer. When the dates are ready, spread them over the bread, and then finish with the other 6 slices of bread.

Whisk the eggs and egg yolks along with the caster sugar. Scrape the vanilla seeds into this mixture and whisk like crazy. Heat the cream along with the empty vanilla pod until just starting to boil. When the eggs are light and voluminous, pour the scalding cream on top and stir with a wooden spoon. Then pour this mixture onto the bread and date layers and leave to soak for at least half an hour. You may have to press down a bit.

Preheat the oven to 170°C.

Sprinkle the demerara sugar over the pudding before baking for about 25 minutes. It will still be a bit wobbly in the centre but should be a gorgeous golden brown. Don't overcook it or it will lose the lovely soft and silky quality. So err on the side of less cooking time as the custard base will keep on cooking even when it's removed from the oven.

Meanwhile make the toffee sauce: heat the butter, syrup and sugar in a small non-stick saucepan until the sugar has melted and it's a thick but fairly smooth paste. Take off the heat and whisk in the crème fraîche. Be careful as it may splutter a bit. The sauce will keep for a few days in the fridge, no bother.

Pour the toffee sauce on the custard base while still warm and serve with a big blob of whipped cream.

TIP: Bicarbonate of soda is added to the dates when they're simmering to help them break down more easily. It makes the water alkaline, which makes vegetables and fruits go 'mushy' with prolonged boiling. This is perfect for what you're trying to achieve in this recipe: a delicious, dry, date mush, to sandwich in between layers of buttery bread.

Apple and polenta cake

Serves 4–6

6 large apples, Cox's or Braeburn

75 g caster sugar

Good tsp cinnamon

125 g coarse polenta

200 g flour

1 tsp baking powder

150 g butter

1 egg

80 ml milk

2 tbsp demerara sugar

I am not, by any stretch, a natural baker, so when I do find a recipe that produces fine results I am quite simply delighted with myself. This recipe was adapted from one of Nigel Slater's in his book Tender (Volume II). It was originally for rhubarb, which for some reason I found nigh impossible to get. Naturally, having bought the polenta, I was determined to have a go at the cake, rhubarb or no rhubarb, so used apple instead. The result was lovely, but I felt it needed a little more sweetness. So – and this is not obligatory – drizzling this cake with the toffee sauce from the previous recipe for sticky toffee pudding is a marriage made in heaven. If you don't want to do the toffee sauce, then add an extra 100 g caster sugar to the polenta and flour mixture to sweeten the cake mix.

This cake can even sit in the fridge for a few days and still taste great. A really fantastic and dead-easy cake.

Preheat the oven to 180°C. Line the base of a 20 cm spring-form cake tin with parchment paper. Grease the sides.

The apples, when peeled, cored and chopped, should total between 500 and 600 g. Toss them in a bowl with the caster sugar and cinnamon. In a food processor, whizz the polenta, flour and baking powder. Add lumps of the butter to make a breadcrumb texture after more pulse whizzing. Then add the egg and milk to form a soft but very sticky dough. Spread two-thirds of the cake mix into the cake tin. Spread the apples on top. Then dot the remaining third of cake mix over the apples. It really is sticky, so do this patchwork style, but as evenly as you can. Sprinkle with the demerara sugar.

Bake for about 40 minutes until a pale golden brown and a skewer comes out clean. It's delicious when it cools down to room temperature and is even better with a drizzle of the toffee sauce. Mmm.

Plum bars

Makes 12–14

550 g plums (about 7–8 plums), stoned

¾ tsp mixed spice

250 g light muscovado sugar

Black pepper

450 g butter

4 tbsp golden syrup

500 g oats

100 g plain flour

50 g chopped walnuts

These plum bars are particularly easy and very tasty. The first time I made them, I was worried that the plums would be a bit pappy, as you just roughly chop them and don't peel them or anything. But they disintegrated to become this lovely layer of jammy, plummy fruitiness between blankets of buttery oats.

Roughly chop the plums and mix with the mixed spice, 75 g of the soft brown sugar and a few grinds of black pepper. Leave to macerate while you prepare the topping. Melt the butter with the rest of the brown sugar (175 g) and the golden syrup. Mix the oats, flour and walnuts together in a big bowl. When the butter mixture is smooth, pour on top of the oats and flour and mix well.

Line a Swiss roll tin measuring 30 x 21 cm with parchment paper and spread half of the oat mixture on the base of the tin, using a spatula that you dip into water to help smooth it down. Spread the plums over and pat down lightly. Then spread the rest of the oat mixture on top, trying to 'seal' in the plums.

Bake at 180°C for about an hour until the topping is golden brown. Allow to cool in the tin for a while and then remove and slice. They keep in an airtight container for a few days.

Lemon and ginger mousse, with lemon and polenta biscuits

Lemon heaven is how some people would describe this dish.

Lemon and ginger mousse

Serves 4

3 small gelatine leaves

4–5 lemons

100 g caster sugar

350 ml cream

2 tbsp stem ginger syrup

Soak the gelatine leaves in cold water until soft. Juice and zest the lemons (you should have approximately 200 ml lemon juice). Heat up half the lemon juice and zest in a small saucepan with the soft gelatine leaves, very gently, until they melt. Do not let it boil or get too hot. Remove from the heat and leave it to cool down. Add the rest of the lemon juice and set aside for a few minutes.

Whisk the sugar and 250 ml of the cream together with the syrup from the stem ginger. When it's starting to get thick, fold in the lemon juice. Keep beating with a whisk, nice and slowly. You may have to cool it down a bit by shoving it in the freezer for 15 minutes and then giving it another whisk. The idea is to chill it down and whisk it to bring it all together so that it becomes thick and voluptuous. At this stage, you should feel the gelatine starting to work. When you do, whisk in the remaining 100 ml of cream to taste.

Spoon into glasses or ramekins and chill down until ready to serve.

Lemon and polenta biscuits

75 g butter

150 g polenta

75 g plain flour

50 g caster sugar

Zest of 1 lemon

1 egg

1 tsp vanilla extract

Extra flour and caster sugar for dusting

Process the butter, polenta, flour, sugar and lemon zest together in a food processor until it resembles sandy breadcrumbs. Add the egg and vanilla extract. It should come together to form a dough. If it doesn't, add a splash of cream or water. Wrap the dough in clingfilm and chill.

When you are ready to bake, preheat the oven to 190°C. Have two baking trays ready and lined with parchment paper. Break off small pieces of the cookie dough and roll into balls, about the size of ping-pong balls. Roll very lightly using some flour and some caster sugar until they flatten down. You need to be able to transfer them onto the baking sheets, but it's best to do this with a non-stick fish slice. The dough should make sixteen to twenty biscuits.

Bake for 15 minutes or so, but do keep an eye on them. They will just start to go golden brown, but they are nicer when they are cooked through but retain their lovely yellow colour, so, if necessary, turn down the oven and cook for a bit longer. It all depends how thick they end up after rolling out.

Allow to cool on a wire rack, and serve with the mousse and, if you fancy them, some macerated strawberries.

Cranberry, strawberry and crunchy granola tart

There are some recipes you look at and think, 'No way!' My declaration that we were going to make this American recipe prompted just this reaction from my sister. Like most American recipes, the quantities had first to be converted for us European metric-centrics (the www.convert-me.com website is brilliant for this). Once that mathematical heartache was over, there followed a good deal of humming and hawing about whether the whole thing would be too sickly sweet. It sounded like a hideous prospect, but the colour looked so great, and I'm so fond of other recipes in this book I've been exploiting (Laurent Tourondel's *Fresh from the Market*), that I felt we should give it a whirl. The resulting tart is really unusual and delicious. Served at room temperature with a good dollop of whipped cream or Greek yoghurt, it surpassed all expectations and looked seriously impressive. Once you get over the initial hump of there being several parts to it, you'll find it's really very do-able.

Serves 6

1 kg strawberries, hulled and roughly chopped

100 g caster sugar

1 tbsp cornstarch

300 g dried cranberries

Zest of 2 oranges

Pastry:

200 g flour

2 tsp caster sugar

120 g butter

Granola:

70 g cornflakes

100 g oats

50 g flaked almonds

1 tsp cinnamon

80 ml olive oil

2 tbsp honey

50 ml maple syrup

1 tsp vanilla extract

Zest of 1 orange

Cook the strawberries in a non-stick saucepan with 100 ml water and 100 g sugar. After about 15 minutes, strain into a clean bowl and push out the juice using a wooden spoon; try to extract as much as possible. Discard the pulp and put the juice back into the saucepan (which you may need to give a quick rinse) and place over a gentle heat. Mix the cornstarch in a cup with a small bit of cold water and, when smooth, whisk it into the strawberry juice. After a few minutes, you'll feel the mixture start to thicken. Remove from the heat and stir in the cranberries and zest. Set aside to cool to room temperature.

Preheat the oven to 200°C.

In a food processor, mix all the pastry ingredients on pulse, then put on full until the pastry just comes together. Sometimes a splash of cream will help this to happen. Wrap in a ball of clingfilm and chill. Then roll out, line a 23 cm tart tin (with a removable base) and chill again if you can. Prick the base and bake for about 15 minutes. Remove the layer of paper and clingfilm/beans and then bake for another few minutes until the pastry is really dry and golden brown. Set aside while you make the granola topping.

Turn down the oven to 140°C. Line a baking sheet with parchment paper. Mix together the cornflakes, oats and almonds. Sprinkle with the cinnamon, and mix. In a small saucepan, bring the oil, honey and maple syrup to the boil. Add the vanilla extract and orange zest. Then pour over the dry ingredients and mix as best you can with a spatula. Spread out onto the parchment paper when it's cool enough to handle, and bake for about 15 minutes. Allow to cool down and then break up to use on top of the tart.

Now you can assemble the tart by simply pouring the strawberry and cranberry compote into the tart shell and topping with a layer of granola. Serve at room temperature or put it in the oven until it is bubbling and warm, about 15 minutes at 160°C, but keep an eye on the granola topping.

Rhubarb curd yoghurt ice cream, with ginger and brown sugar meringues and rhubarb compote

Rhubarb is such a delicious fruit, although technically it's a vegetable. Originally native to Asia, eventually it filtered over to Britain in the sixteenth century, where it was valued for its medicinal qualities, especially its ability to settle the stomach and (ahem) its 'purgative' qualities, which sounds a bit nicer than 'mild laxative'. It made its way into tarts and pies in the 1800s, and today it's one of Ireland's favourite crumble and pie fillings.

This recipe offers what I can only describe as a rhubarb 'feast'! There's a rhubarb curd that is used to make a dead simple ice cream (from *Leith's Seasonal Bible*), some brown sugar meringues (which send me hurtling back to the 1980s) and a very straightforward rhubarb compote to blob on top. Make one or all three recipes. They go superbly together or are delicious on their own.

Rhubarb curd yoghurt ice cream

Serves 4–6

300 g chopped, prepared rhubarb stems

2 tsp stem ginger in syrup, finely chopped

4 egg yolks, beaten

170 g caster sugar

110 g butter, cut into cubes

290 ml Greek yoghurt

Put the rhubarb in a saucepan with 50 ml water, cover with a lid and gently poach until it breaks down. Pass through a sieve to extract all the lovely rhubarb juice. Mush it with the back of a wooden spoon rather than a metal spoon so as not impart a metallic taste. In a clean saucepan, preferably non-stick, heat the rhubarb juice along with the chopped ginger, egg yolks, sugar and butter. Mix really well and eventually it will thicken enough to coat the back of a spoon. Season with more ginger syrup or sugar if necessary. Allow to cool, then stir in the yoghurt, mix well and freeze in a plastic container for a few hours or overnight.

Ginger and brown sugar meringues

4 egg whites

30 g caster sugar

150 g demerara sugar

1 tsp ground ginger

Preheat the oven to 140°C. Cover two baking sheets with baking parchment.

Whisk the egg whites until stiff. Add the caster sugar and whisk until shiny. Fold in the brown sugar and ginger. Put 5 big blobs of meringue mixture onto each tray and bake for about an hour. Allow them to cool before peeling off.

Rhubarb compote

300 g chopped, prepared rhubarb stems

Juice of 1 lemon

Zest and juice of 1 orange

2 tbsp caster sugar

2 tbsp stem ginger syrup

This couldn't be simpler. Heat up all the ingredients until soft but still a bit chunky. Check the seasoning. Allow to cool and spoon this onto anything and everything you fancy.

TIP: I found that in one recipe, 450 g of rhubarb stems yielded 300 g of nicely chopped bits of firm rhubarb, but in another, it took 600 g of stalks to yield 300 g. It really depends on the shape the rhubarb is in. It's not fond of any sort of heat, so will wilt and disintegrate more quickly if old and left out. Allow roughly double the quantity of rhubarb stems for the appropriate amount of prepped stems.

Toffee popcorn

Serves 5–10

75 g corn kernels
2 tbsp sunflower oil
50 g butter
50 g soft brown sugar
2 tbsp golden syrup
Good pinch salt

I have to confess that before this recipe, I had never made toffee popcorn. I found it on the dear old internet where, needless to say, there are plenty of recipes to choose from. My sister Peaches and I agree that what we've come up with is the right balance of buttery sweetness and salty corn. We found it very hard to stop eating it – it's unbelievably moreish. Perfect for when you want to curl up on the sofa and veg out en masse.

In a heavy-based saucepan with a lid, heat up the corn in the sunflower oil. Swirl it around so the corn is well coated and then put the lid on, keep the heat medium and wait until you start to hear some popping. Turn down the heat a bit and keep the lid on. At this stage the popping should gain some momentum. You can give the pan a little shake (but please do keep the lid on!) and keep on the heat until you think you've enough heat to keep it going. It usually takes about 10 to 15 minutes from start to finish. If you find they haven't all popped, then leave the unpopped ones in, remove the layer of popcorn and heat again with the lid on for longer.

Put the popcorn in a huge bowl. Meanwhile, have your butter, sugar and golden syrup warming until the butter has melted and the sugar has dissolved. Pour this hot mixture onto the corn. With a spatula, mix and fold the popcorn around the bowl. Eventually all will be well coated. Sprinkle with salt and keep mixing and folding. Taste and add more salt if necessary. Serve straightaway.

Hot chocolate

Serves 8–10

270 g dark chocolate
270 g milk chocolate
500 ml cream
1 litre milk
3–4 tbsp caster sugar
4 tbsp dark rum (optional)
Extra whipped cream and chocolate shavings for decoration

Who doesn't love hot chocolate? Well, if you've forgotten its simple pleasures (and believe me, children always remember them), this version will bring them all back, being particularly delicious and decadent – even without the optional splash of rum for the grown-ups, which works a treat. It might seem a bit boring, but let me tell you, this is good stuff, especially after a brisk walk on a cool day.

Break the chocolate into a large bowl. Heat the cream and milk until just about to boil. Pour onto the chocolate, carefully, mix well with a wooden spoon and add the sugar if you think it's a bit bitter. Serve as is, or add the rum. Top with blobs of softly whipped cream and chocolate shavings, or not.

acknowledgments

Joanne Murphy for her gorgeous pictures and years of friendship. I love your work!

Orla Neligan for an unending supply of beautiful props and her fabulous sense of style.

Carly Horan – the new kid on the block – for assisting on the shoot and being such a pro.

Paul Kavanagh for excellent cooking and prep skills and saving many dishes from the destruction and havoc that I wreak.

Gillian Fallon for pulling together and helping to pluck four years' worth of recipes and to shape them into something resembling a book. A great editing job.

Ivan Mulcahy in MCA and all in Gill & Macmillan for making this entire process an awful lot easier than it should be, especially Nicki, Catherine, Jennifer, Don, Ciara and Teresa.

The Irish Times for putting up with me week in week out, especially Marie Claire and Rachel, and their wonderful editors Orna and formerly Patsey. Thanks also to all the *Irish Times* photographers, who are incredibly patient and great at what they do.

My friends and family who have to put up with plenty of botched recipes, burnt dinners and bad moods. I love sitting down at the table with you.

Peaches – sister, business partner and friend – the list of things to thank you for is far too great. I wouldn't be here if it weren't for you!

And finally to my husband, Garvan, and our two girls, Lauren and Maeve. From the bottom of my heart, thank you, thank you, thank you.

Irish Times food writer Domini Kemp trained as a chef at Leith's in London before opening the hugely popular itsa food company with her sister, Peaches, in 1999. There are now six branches of the itsa stores and two itsa cafés. They also run Table restaurant in Brown Thomas, Cork, The Restaurant in Brown Thomas, Dublin, and the catering company, Feast. They have recently opened The Tea Rooms in Dublin Castle.

Domini regularly contributes to TV, magazines and newspapers. This is her third cookbook.

Praise for Domini's previous book, *Itsa Cookbook*:

'You'll find Domini Kemp's sense of style, taste and humour in every one of these recipes.'
The Irish Times

'With loads of quick and easy recipes and inspirational photography that had us driven demented with hunger at lunchtime, we think Domini's tome is a sure-fire winner.'
Image Magazine

'Will appeal to anyone looking for tasty and healthy food ideas to fit into their hectic schedules.'
Sunday Business Post